50 Days

Of

Elevation

PISHON GROVE PUBLISHING

©2022 by Shamika Rich, Pishon Grove Publishing

Published by Pishon Grove Publishing
Albany, Ga. 31705

www.shamikarich.com

Printed in the United States of America

ISBN 979-8-9902978-1-4
Scripture is taken from the King James Version® and is marked KJV: King James Version public domain.
Scripture is taken from the New King James Version®. Copyright © 1982 by Thomas Nelson. They are used by permission. All rights reserved. Scripture quotations marked (AMP) are taken from the Amplified Bible, Copyright © 1954, 1958, 1962, 1964, 1965, 1987 by The Lockman Foundation. They are used by permission.
Scripture quotations marked TPT are from The Passion Translation®. Copyright © 2017, 2018 by Passion & Fire Ministries, Inc. Used by permission. All rights reserved. ThePassionTranslation.com.

CONTENTS

DEDICATION

I dedicate this body of work to the Lord Jesus. My family and the laborers of Titus two ministries. My patient, loving and supportive husband who moves mountains for me. For the many mornings he covered his head with the pillow and covers trying to sleep but found himself covering me while in prayer. The praise and worship music played unapologetically every morning at six a.m. and immediately after, it was right into the prayer, and then a twenty-to-thirty-minute teaching. Prayer was loud, fervent, and for so many believers gathered on one line, one place, with unique needs, but all wanting a touch from our Lord and savior Christ Jesus the anointed one. Thank you, My Anthony, for the many sacrifices you made for me to obey the voice and call of God! May I repay you with retirement? Most of all hubby thank you for waiting for me. I also dedicate these writings to my children. They have shared me with so many people and with the ministry. Thank you, children, for serving with dad and I in ministry. I felt most strong with all of you by my side. In my push to complete this work my goal was to leave a legacy of work for you all. Share these writings with your children. I write to the prophet and priest in all of you, because one day a time will come when you must go through these stages of spiritual elevation for yourself. My prayer is that whether I am present or absent it will be a blueprint for you to navigate your life in Christ.

Psalm 24

¹ The earth *is* the Lord's, and all that therein is the world and they that dwell therein.

² For he hath founded it upon the [a]seas; and established it upon the floods.

³ Who shall ascend into the mountain of the Lord? and who shall stand in his holy place?

⁴ *Even he that hath* innocent hands, and a pure heart, which hath not lifted his mind unto vanity, nor sworn deceitfully.

⁵ He shall receive a blessing from the Lord, and righteousness from the God of his salvation.

⁶ This is the [b]generation of them that seek him, of them that seek thy face, *this is* Jacob. Selah.

⁷ [c]Lift up your heads ye gates, and be ye lifted up ye everlasting doors, and the King of glory shall come in.

⁸ Who is this King of glory? the Lord, strong and mighty, *even* the Lord mighty in battle.

⁹ Lift up your heads, ye gates, and lift up *yourselves* ye everlasting doors, and the King of glory shall come in.

¹⁰ Who is this King of glory? the Lord of hosts, he is the King of glory. Selah.

INTRODUCTION

As we explore the depth of our lives, who we are and who we desire to be, we must establish a fresh start. A fresh start mentally, physically, and emotionally is needed. I call this your stride, and we will explore this topic more. During these **50 days of Elevation,** my intention is to help you understand what spiritual elevation is and to lead you to ascend that you may partner with the Holy Spirit in your everyday life, revealing outwardly His plan and purposes. My desire is to help you identify areas in your life and your daily habits that may be hindering you from living a dynamic spiritual life.

Welcome to your now! This is the place you find yourself presently while reading this body of work. Yep, you are here, and you are not alone! If you are willing, if you are afraid, apprehensive, or experiencing plain ole tired enough is enough.

Then yes sir, yes ma'am, you picked up or downloaded the right book. You are exactly where you need to be.

If, in fact, you have been feeling any of the emotions that were just described, then let's go! It is time to make some assessments. Would you do something for me? Inhale, now exhale. Please do this as many times as needed. This process is called ex-spelling. Come on, one for the Father, the Son, and the Holy Spirit! You may need to repeat this process over the next fifty days. No worries go right ahead. You should be feeling some relief after releasing some worries and anxieties or even anger and discontentment you may have been carrying.

Thoughts Of Virtue is your personal journal included at the end of every day. It is crucial to document your progress, your feelings, and identify other issues that may otherwise be difficult to speak out loud. I have learned since I was a young girl that writing what I could not speak was therapeutic in my growth and development.

I have also included **scriptures** for you to meditate on; I found this to be so helpful each year as we embarked upon 50 days of elevation.

I would like to include the fasting regimen we were on, but because of dietary or health reasons, it is better to check with your doctor before altering your diet, especially if you take medication. We fasted according to our blood type: Meaning from 6:00 AM to 6:00 PM we ate according to our blood type; we chose specific juicing and smoothie recipes that coincided with that specific blood type, A, B, AB, or O positive or negative. Those who participated had tremendous testimonies starting around week 2, but many did not stay the course. Fasting, in my opinion, is the greatest asset to the 50-day journey of developing your spiritual, emotional, and physical stride in life. May You find joy and fulfillment as you embark upon your elevation. If you find yourself falling off the wagon as we all did over the last five years, please get up the next day and get back in the race. This is about the grace of God to help you finish well, not your ability to be in control.

Yours, in Christ
Mika,

RESET

Welcome to day one of the fifty days of elevation!

As we embark on this journey of self-discovery and growth, it is important to first confront the harsh reality of our current situation. Reality may not always be pleasant but facing it head-on is the first step towards making real and lasting changes.

To begin this process, let us first understand the meaning of the term "reset". According to the dictionary, resetting means to set again or start anew. It is restoring something to its original, pristine state. We can see this in action when we reset our phones or clocks, bringing them back to their original factory settings. What do you think about resetting our lives? How do we start anew and restore our lives to their original, unadulterated state? The answer lies in taking a deep breath, reflecting on our life, and taking ownership of our part in it all.

As we embark on this course of self-examination, I am reminded of the words from the book of Philippians, *"Do not be anxious about anything, but in every situation, by prayer and petition, with thanksgiving, present your requests to God"* (4:6). This verse reminds us to let go of our worries and trust in God to guide us.

Resetting our lives is not just about getting rid of the negative aspects, but also about finding ways to invigorate and elevate our lives. It is like sorting through the nooks and crannies of our hearts, but with a mustard seed of faith. We need to take a closer look at our thoughts, habits, and actions and make necessary changes to align them with our goals and values. It may not be an easy process, but it is necessary for our personal growth and happiness. Embrace this day of resetting and prepare for the journey ahead. Trust in the process and believe that we have the strength and resilience to overcome any challenges that may come our way.

In the next forty-nine days, we will delve deeper into various aspects of our lives and explore ways to elevate them, but for now, on day one, let us take a moment to reset and prepare for what is coming. Remember, it is never too late to start anew and create the life we truly desire.

Thoughts Of Virtue

EXAMINE YOURSELF? WHAT IS HOLDING YOU BACK?

_____

_____

_____

_____

_____

_____

_____

_____

_____

_____

_____

_____

Be anxious for nothing, but in everything by prayer and supplication, with thanksgiving, let your requests be made known to God; 7 and the peace of God, which surpasses all understanding, will guard your hearts and minds through Christ Jesus

Philippians 4:6-7

ASSESSMENT

Welcome back to the second day of 50 days of elevation.

Today, we are going to discuss something that can be emotionally overwhelming - assessing the damage in our lives. Do not worry, you are not alone in this. Think about a disaster.

Maybe you have experienced one firsthand or have seen it on the news. Whether it is a tornado, hurricane, mudslide, wildfire, divorce, death, or traumatic experience, - these powerful, uncontrollable forces can devastate entire lives, communities, and families. When life throws a catastrophic event your way, it can feel just like that - a disaster. Everything you thought was rock solid suddenly became shattered. You are left to sift through the rubble, feeling lost and clueless about what comes next. Tears stream down your face and your body shivers as you try to make sense of the chaos that surrounds you. How could you not be affected?

This happens when the storms of life hit us. They have a history of disrupting everything in their path. As humans, we feel overwhelmed and broken when the storms of life hit us. We try to avoid facing the harsh reality of our storms, but eventually, we must assess the damage done.

In moments like these, it is hard to see any hope or light at the end of the tunnel. It makes us wonder how we will ever rebuild what has been destroyed. After every storm, hope arises from an unwavering and steadfast place. *Isaiah 25:4 says, "For you have been a stronghold to the poor, a stronghold to the needy in his distress, a shelter from the storm and a shade from the heat; for the breath of the ruthless is like a storm against a wall."* This verse reminds us that during our storms, there is a stronghold, a shelter, and a shade to which we can run. That stronghold is Christ, the solid rock. When we anchor our hope and faith in Christ, we can weather any storm. We may still feel the effects of it, but we know that we are not alone. As we assess the damage of our lives, we can lean on the Holy Spirit, who will guide us and give us the strength to rebuild.

There is one thing we must remember - the storm will pass. Just like a physical storm, the storms of life eventually come to an end. When it does, we will have a stronger foundation, a deeper faith, and a greater appreciation for the goodness and faithfulness of God. I hope you are ready to clean up the chaos after assessing the damage. It will not be easy but know that you are not alone. With hope and faith in Christ, and the guidance of the Holy Spirit, you can rebuild and come out stronger. You are a conqueror and an overcomer. Keep standing on Christ, who is the solid rock, and know that you are loved and never alone.

Thoughts Of Virtue

HOW DID I SURVIVE THAT STORM?

_____

_____

_____

_____

_____

_____

_____

_____

_____

_____

_____

_____

_____

For thou hast been a strength to the poor, a strength to the needy in his distress, a refuge from the storm, a shadow from the heat, when the blast of the terrible ones is as a storm against the wall.

Isaiah 25:4

SIFTING

Welcome to day three of our fifty days of elevation journey.

I am glad you are here, and I am even more grateful that you are asking this question: *Can anything good come out of this?* I am here to tell you that yes, absolutely, something amazing can come out of this. This stage may seem exhausting, it may seem like you are all alone, or that all hope is lost. I would like to share a profound script*ure from Ecclesiastes 3:11, "He has made everything beautiful in its time. He has also set eternity in the human heart; yet no one can fathom what God has done from beginning to end."*

Take a moment to let that sink in. You see, this stage holds a beautiful aspect. It is like the remnants of a beautiful home after a major storm that has been torn, scattered, or even flooded in some cases. It may seem messy and chaotic, but it is up to you to start sifting through those remnants to find the hidden beauty within them.

I know it may not be an easy task. Sifting through the pieces of ourselves that remain after facing difficult situations takes patience, courage, and strength, but someone has to do it, and that someone is you.

Do not let yourself get derailed by those who are not present during this stage. They may never come to aid or help you during this process, and that is okay. In fact, it may even present an opportunity for you to discover something or someone new. This stage is about you sifting so you can repurpose what remains, so sifting is very important, and this stage can be tedious, but necessary, and exciting.

I encourage you to prepare yourself emotionally. Take a deep breath and reflect on what you can repurpose in this season. What can you revive? Think about any gifts or talents that may have been buried under the weight of past experiences. Write your vision and make it clear, so that when the time is right, you can pursue it with all your heart. Life is a journey, and sometimes we must go through the process of sifting through the remnants, the broken pieces, to find the true beauty within ourselves. It takes patience and trust, but in the end, it is always worth it.

My dear friend, do not lose hope. Embrace this stage and the fresh start it offers. Take advantage of the process of sifting and remember, God has a beautiful plan for your life, and *He will make everything beautiful in its time.* Keep going and believe that something amazing and transformative will come out of this.

Thoughts Of Virtue

CAN ANYTHING GOOD COME OUT OF THIS?

_____

_____

_____

_____

_____

_____

_____

_____

_____

_____

_____

_____

So, from now on we regard no one according to the flesh. although we once regarded Christ in this way, we do so no longer. [17]Therefore if anyone is in Christ, he is a new creation. The old has passed away. Behold, the new has come!

2 Cor 5:16

REPURPOSING

Congratulations, you have made it to day four of fifty days of elevation!

As you clean up and assess, you may have discovered a thought: *"What do I have that I can reuse?"* You may have even dismissed this idea, thinking it is not worth your time or effort. Before you toss something useful aside, let me introduce you to the skill of repurposing. *Repurposing is the art of transforming something old or worn into a fresh, new piece.* It is a powerful skill to have, and it is all about looking at things in a new and creative light. Before you bulldoze your way through and start fresh with a clean slate, consider the potential of what you already have.

Life can often feel like a never-ending string of moments, right before your breakthrough. Can you relate? In these moments, it is not unusual to forget the importance of our prefixes–*What was there before*, but trust me, everything you confront and assess can play a crucial role in shaping your next chapters in life. Now, you may wonder, why should you trust me? What do I know about your life's prefixes? Let me offer you some comfort as we navigate through the clutter in your mind, heart, and soul. Think of me as a personal assistant, helping you sift through the hidden rooms and corridors of your life.

With the guidance of the Holy Spirit, we can make sense of it all and see how it ties into your now. Yes, it may sound overwhelming, and there may be moments of resistance, but I assure you it will be worth it. As you come to understand the prefix of where it began, where it went wrong, where it stalled out, then and only then are you in the right posture to elevate into new realms. Let me explain. You can't elevate beyond what you are not willing to confront. I have a saying," Are you elevating or deflating"? Remember, repurposing is not just about materials or objects. It applies to our spiritual, emotional, and physical health and well-being also. Repurposing in this phase is about acknowledging that I can take what was meant to break me to build me. I can take what was meant to stiff me to gift me, what was meant to discourage me to flourish me or someone else for that matter. As you commit to this process of elevation, you will embrace the power of creative miracles through repurposing. Some of the most notable members of society, small business owners, actors, and actresses, quiet millionaires and billionaires were born through this stage. what do I have in my hands that I can use. Speak to every gift and every old or new dream so that it can live.

I may not know the exact details of your life, but I am here to offer you comfort, motivation, inspiration, and support.

Thoughts Of Virtue

WHAT DO I HAVE THAT I CAN USE AGAIN?

_____

_____

_____

_____

_____

_____

_____

_____

_____

_____

Therefore, since we have been justified by faith, we have peace with God through our Lord Jesus Christ. Through him we have also obtained access by faith into this grace in which we stand, and we rejoice in hope of the glory of God. More than that, we rejoice in our sufferings, knowing that suffering produces endurance, and endurance produces character, and character produces hope, and hope does not put us to shame, because God's love has been poured into our hearts through the Holy Spirit who has been given to us.

Romans 5:1-5

TRANSFORMATION

Can you believe it is already day 5 of 50 days of elevation?

You have almost made it through the week. Today, I want you to take a moment to reflect on your journey so far. Let us be honest, transformation is divinely becoming who God intended for you to be from the moment you were created. Consider this, you have committed to work on you for once in your life. That may mean, you chose to leave behind all the ugliness, brokenness, hurt, craziness that once occupied your life to get here. In this place, you discover the hard truths about yourself. You come out stronger, more resilient, and now you become something and someone brand new. You shine with the Glory of God, and trust me, you do not even need to shout it from the rooftops. People will start to notice the change in you.

This is the moment where what was meant to break and destroy you becomes the very stage for your grand performance. Stand tall and share your testimony with the audience of life. Do you recognize this place? It is unlike any other you have experienced on this earth. I want to remind you of something, this elevation may be uncomfortable. It may push you to your limits and make you disconnect from anything that no longer serves the best part of you and who you are becoming. It is all part of the process, because only when we die to unhealthy desires can we be restored through Christ Jesus.

Do not be afraid of transformation, it is much like the cocoon of a caterpillar. Embrace the unknown, the discomfort, the challenges, and the victories. Through it all, you are becoming the best version of yourself, and emerging as a beautiful colorful butterfly, it is all going to be worth it in the end.

Keep pushing, keep growing, keep elevating. Always remember, this journey is not just about you. Your transformation and elevation will inspire those around you, as well as generations to come.

Thoughts Of Virtue

I'M RESETTING MY LIFE SO I CAN ELEVATE FOR GENERATIONS
TO COME.

_____

_____

_____

_____

_____

_____

_____

_____

_____

_____

_____

_____

Now the mind of the flesh is death [both now and forever because it pursues sin]; but the mind of the Spirit is life and peace [the spiritual well-being that comes from walking with God—both now and forever]; ⁷ the mind of the flesh [with its sinful pursuits] is actively hostile to God.

Romans 8:6

DIE TO YOURSELF

Welcome to day six.

This is the only way for you to ascend into the hill of the Lord. These 50 days of self-sacrifice will unfortunately be attached to some daily death. With that being said, let us not prolong your elevation for today.

Romans 8:5 for those who are living according to the flesh set their minds on the things of the flesh [which gratify the body], but those who are living according to the Spirit, [set their minds on] the things of the Spirit [His will and purpose]. ⁶ Now the mind of the flesh is death [both now and forever—because it pursues sin]; but the mind of the Spirit is life and peace [the spiritual well-being that comes from walking with God—both now and forever]; ⁷ the mind of the flesh [with its sinful pursuits] is actively hostile to God. It does not submit itself to God's law, since it cannot, ⁸ and those who are in the flesh [living a life that caters to sinful appetites and impulses] cannot please God.

⁹ However, you are not [living] in the flesh [controlled by the sinful nature] but in the Spirit, if in fact the Spirit of God lives in you [directing and guiding you]. But if anyone does not have the Spirit of Christ, he does not belong to Him [and is not a child of God]. ¹⁰ If Christ lives in you, though your [natural] body is dead because of sin, your spirit is alive because of righteousness [which He provides].

Let us look at a few meanings of righteousness.

1: acting in accord with divine or moral law: free from guilt or sin. 2. morally right or justifiable a righteous decision.

Righteousness is one of the chief attributes of God, as portrayed in the Hebrew Bible. Its chief meaning concerns **ethical conduct** (for example, *Leviticus 19:36; Deuteronomy 25:1; Psalm 1:6; Proverbs 8:20)*. In the Book of Job, Job is introduced to us as a person who is perfect in righteousness. We soon come to realize as we study the life of Job that his righteousness was put on the auction block.

Job 1:6 One day as the angels came to present themselves before the Lord, Satan, the Accuser, came with them.[7] "Where have you come from?" the Lord asks Satan. And Satan replies, "From earth, where I've been watching everything that's going on."[8] Then the Lord asks Satan, "Have you noticed my servant, Job? He is the finest man in all the earth—a good man who fears God and will have nothing to do with evil."

[9] *"Why shouldn't he when you pay him so well?" Satan scoffs.* [10] *"You have always protected him and his home and his property from all harm. You have prospered everything he does—look how rich he is! No wonder he 'worships' you!* [11] *But just take away his wealth, and you will see him curse you to your face!"*[12-13] *And the Lord replies to Satan, "You may do anything you like with his wealth, but don't harm him physically. "So, Satan went away; and sure enough, not long afterwards when Job's sons and daughters were dining at the oldest brother's house, tragedy struck.*

"Tragedy, at times, can be seen as the Lord's way of showcasing our ability to overcome challenges and emphasizing His absolute power over Satan. Let me explain further. When everything in our lives goes smoothly, we may not think about our personal relationship with the Lord. Prayers are often inconsistent unless we are facing difficulties or need answers. That is when we may call for a fast or pray fervently to experience a breakthrough; however, Job's children were not like this. Scripture does not mention them honoring the Lord. Instead, we see Job making sacrifices for them after their days of partying and drinking.

In a similar way, some of our own children may want nothing to do with church or our faith practices, finding them excessive and too time-consuming. They prefer spending time with friends and enjoying the blessings readily available to them. The beginning of Job teaches us that even when Satan did not have permission to harm Job and his family, he was always watching. It was only when the Lord removed His hedge of protection that Satan could touch them. In the Old Testament, we see generations who knew the historical accounts but lacked a personal relationship with God. Simply put, they lacked a true connection."

Thoughts Of Virtue

WHO/WHAT HAVE I SPRITUALLY BEEN CONNECTED TO?

_____

_____

_____

_____

_____

_____

_____

_____

_____

_____

_____

_____

_____

Then the Lord asks Satan, "Have you noticed my servant, Job? He is the finest man in all the earth—a good man[e] who fears God and will have nothing to do with evil."

Job1:8

WHO GOT NEXT?

You made it to day seven.

Imagine if relationships were at the core of being a servant. In the book of Job, Satan suggested that Job only worshipped God because of his possessions. God revealed that Job's devotion came from his heart to serve. Throughout the bible, we see Job's determination to follow God's commandments and please Him. Think back to those times when you were passionately seeking God and striving to please Him. Be comforted that sometimes our trials are God and Jesus bragging about us to the devil.

Do you realize how much God values your heart and honor towards Him? Well, so much so that He may allow a test to come your way just to prove it, but rest assured, God has set boundaries, and no test, that The Lord has permitted, can take your life. Think back to those moments in your life where you were tested but felt God's protection and guidance or not.

Write them down and reflect on how you came to see the hand of God through those tests. We can gain insight from the mistakes of the next generation after Joshua and Caleb. They rejected the spiritual principles of covenant reciprocity and chose to do things their own way. During their struggles, they learned to cry out to God for help, so let us to learn from our struggles and grow in our understanding knowing that although we would like for people to respond to our cry, the reality is everyone has not been sent to deliver us. I have seen countless biblical encounters where God's children cried, and the almighty God responded as their deliverer.

Thoughts Of Virtue

I KNEW IT WAS GOD PROTECTING ME WHEN:

_____

_____

_____

_____

_____

_____

_____

_____

_____

_____

_____

_____

_____

_____

As far as I am concerned, God turned into good what you meant for evil, for he brought me to this high position I have today so that I could save the lives of many people.

Gen 50:20

THE KEY OF LEGACY

Welcome to day eight of your fifty-day journey.

Let us unlock the door of the benefit and blessing of keeping a standard of covenant alive from one generation to the next. Through trial and error, we will see how the descendants of Caleb navigated through their own personal wilderness experience. Every generation must come to know God for themselves. In Judges, you find the children of Israel in a time of distress, but they knew enough and remembered what to do. They called a fast, and cried out to the Lord, and He answered them. The book of Judges chapter three is one example of this account.

Judges 3:1 Now these are the nations which the Lord left, that He might test Israel by them, that is, all who had not [a]known any of the wars in Canaan ² (this was only so that the generations of the children of Israel might be taught to know war, at least those who had not formerly known it), ³ namely, five lords of the Philistines, all the Canaanites, the Sidonians, and the Hivites who dwelt in Mount Lebanon, from Mount Baal Hermon to the entrance of Hamath. ⁴ And they were left, that He might test Israel by them, to [b]know whether they would obey the commandments of the Lord, which He had commanded their fathers by the hand of Moses. ⁵ Thus the children of Israel dwelt among the Canaanites, the Hittites, the Amorites, the Perizzites, the Hivites, and the Jebusites. ⁶ And they took their daughters to be their wives and gave their daughters to their sons; and they served their gods.

[7] So the children of Israel did evil in the sight of the Lord. They forgot the Lord their God, and served the Baals and [c]Asherah. [8] Therefore the anger of the Lord was hot against Israel, and He sold them into the hand of Cushan-Rishathaim king of Mesopotamia; and the children of Israel served Cushan-Rishathaim eight years. [9] When the children of Israel cried out to the Lord, the Lord raised up a deliverer for the children of Israel, who delivered them: Othniel the son of Kenaz, Caleb's younger brother. [10] The Spirit of the Lord came upon him, and he judged Israel. He went out to war, and the Lord delivered Cushan-Rishathaim king of Mesopotamia into his hand; and his hand prevailed over Cushan-Rishathaim. [11] So the land had rest for forty years. Then Othniel the son of Kenaz died.

I pray that through this passage in Judges, you can see how tragedy can produce prayer in a whole generation. Was it tragic for that generation to inter-marry? Not at first, it seemed like the thing to do. Until they took on the practices of the ones they married, erecting unholy altars of idolatry through the worship of Baal and Asherah. Could it be that what you are worshipping has caused sin to abound in your life? What practices have you taken on that are contrary to your Christian belief? Let us repent and renounce those things that you may have picked up and ask the Lord Jesus to deliver you and your house as you cry out from a place of desperation. Say this prayer aloud.

Prayer Of Repentance and Renunciation

Father, I repent for every unholy practice that I participated in, knowingly or unknowingly. Every covenant that is unholy, I denounce it this day. *Romans 10:9 Jesus come into my life. I receive you and need you as my savior. I believe that you died for me on the cross at calvary and rose from the grave on my behalf.* Break every chain that has held me captive. Destroy every yoke of bondage that has weighed me down. Restore the years that the locust and canker worm ate up concerning my harvest. Jesus, give me back my life. Remove every charm and ticker that was placed in me to track my movement and mobility in the earth. Remove every photo of myself or my family members from unholy altars of every kind, including Baal or Asherah. Any food, drink or blood sacrifice that was used to bind me to the kingdom of darkness uproot it from the deepest and furthest part of my being. Cut every unholy cord that binds me to the kingdom of darkness. To the marine kingdom and any other kingdom, I am un-aware of. Seal my dream realm and prevent witches, warlocks, and all astral activity from controlling or infiltrating my life through the dream. May the cord of every satanic agent be cut in the mighty name of Jesus. Jesus, I ask that you fill every empty place and destroy all works of my flesh with the fruits of the spirit according to your word in Galatians 5:13-26. *That I may walk uprightly before you all the days of my life.*

Thoughts Of Virtue

WHAT DID I WORSHIP IN MY WILDERNESS?

_____

_____

_____

_____

_____

_____

_____

_____

_____

_____

_____

_____

For the weapons of our warfare are not carnal, but mighty through God to the pulling down of strong holds;[5] Casting down imaginations, and every high thing that exalteth itself against the knowledge of God and bringing into captivity every thought to the obedience of Christ.

1 Cor 10:4-5

FIGHT BACK

Welcome to Day 9.

Let us get started. The lust of the flesh is likened to a bully that you keep trying to avoid. The thing with bullies is that if they can manipulate you into never fighting back, or believing you cannot win the fight, they hold the power that you should possess in their hands. This is the mirage of our flesh. When you are under manipulation, which is witchcraft, you don't know what's bullying you. Many times, bullies have no place to go or no one to turn to, so they isolate you to themselves. They are disembodied spirits looking for a house to squat in. It is high time we kicked the squatters out by walking in the Spirit, not fulfilling the lusts of our flesh.

Today, as you reflect on who or what has taken up space in your spiritual house, consider this question: Do you have a legal right to be here? If not, then you must go in the mighty name of Jesus! Now would be a good place to identify things that you may have done or doors you may have opened. If you have engaged in activities such as palm reading, sorcery, astral projection, necromancy, black magic, voodoo, chanting, or any other dark practices, it is possible that you have inadvertently allowed demonic influences to enter your life. To start addressing this, it is important to first acknowledge and identify these unwanted spiritual occupants in your life. This is a prophetic action that requires you to confront any involvement or exposure truthfully and honestly.

Take authority in renouncing them, just as we have done before, and command them to depart in the powerful name of Jesus. As you renounce and expel these entities from your life, you may notice their manifestations. It is common to experience coughing, purging, or a sudden need to visit the restroom during this process, as it is all part of the self-deliverance process.

While this is a good starting point, it is advisable to seek the guidance of a true deliverance minister, who is skilled at assisting you with the finished work that only comes through Christ Jesus.

The thing with bully's is that if they can manipulate you into never fighting back, and or believing you cannot win the fight, they hold the power that you should possess in their hands.

Thoughts Of Virtue

EVERY SQUATTER MUST GO! CALL THEM OUT BY NAME:

_____

_____

_____

_____

_____

_____

_____

_____

_____

_____

_____

_____

_____

Now the works of the flesh[a] are obvious: [b] sexual immorality, impurity, depravity, 20 idolatry, sorcery, [c] hostilities, [d] strife, [e] jealousy, outbursts of anger, selfish rivalries, dissensions, [f] factions, 21 envying, [g] murder,[h] drunkenness, carousing,[i] and similar things. I am warning you, as I had warned you before: Those who practice such things will not inherit the kingdom of God!

Gal 5:19-21

WALK IT OUT

Congratulations on making it to Day 10 of your 50 days of elevation journey. Today's topic is all about walking in the spirit–a vital aspect of our Christian walk.

In Galatians 5:22-26, we are reminded of the fruit of the spirit–love, joy, peace, patience, kindness, goodness, faithfulness, gentleness, and self-control. These are all qualities that should be evident in our lives as we walk in the spirit. But what does it mean to walk in the spirit? Simply put, it means to live our lives under the guidance and influence of the Holy Spirit. This is not an easy task, as we are constantly battling against our fleshly desires and the temptations of the world. Through the power of the Holy Spirit, we can overcome and truly live a life that is pleasing to God.

As Christians, we have been called to crucify our flesh and its passions and desires. This means putting to death our selfish and sinful nature and allowing the Holy Spirit to transform us from the inside out. It is not about following a set of rules or trying to be perfect but surrendering our lives to God and allowing His spirit to work in us.

Walking in the spirit also means living in accordance with the spirit. This involves being conscious of our thoughts, words, and actions, making sure they align with the fruit of the spirit. It is about being led by the spirit instead of being led by our own desires. In this path of walking in the spirit, we must also be mindful of our attitudes towards others. The passage reminds us not to become conceited or to provoke one another, but instead to show love and gentleness towards our brothers and sisters in Christ. We can sometimes fall into the trap of comparing ourselves with others or being jealous of what others have, but as we walk in the spirit, we learn to celebrate each other's victories and support each other in times of need.

My friend, walking in the spirit is a continuous process. It is not something we achieve overnight, but a daily pursuit of surrendering our lives to God and allowing the Holy Spirit to work in us. May we continue this journey of elevation, growing in our faith and cultivating the fruit of the spirit. Remember, as followers of Christ, we are not bound by the law, but by the spirit, therefore let us embrace this new way of living and allow the Holy Spirit to guide us every step of the way. Walk it out through the Spirit and I will meet you on day eleven.

Thoughts Of Virtue

WHERE CAN I APPLY THE 9 GIFTS OF SPIRIT IN MY LIFE?

_____

_____

_____

_____

_____

_____

_____

_____

_____

_____

_____

_____

_____

_____

But the fruit of the Spirit[j] is love,[k] joy, peace, patience, kindness, goodness, faithfulness,[l] 23 gentleness, and[m] self-control. Against such things there is no law.

Gal 5:22-26

COUNT IT ALL JOY

Welcome to Day 11.

There is a powerful lesson to be learned from James, chapter 1. We are encouraged to give thanks for the trials and tribulations that the Lord has brought us through, because during those challenging times, something greater is produced within us. It is through the fires of adversity that our character is shaped and refined. In a world that often views tragedy as something to be avoided at all costs, this perspective may seem contrary when you are directly affected. The scriptures remind us to "count it all joy" when we face various trials. This is not to suggest that we should take surety in pain or suffering, but rather that we can find joy in the growth and transformation that occurs as we navigate through these hardships.

Reflecting on the life of our brother James, we witness a profound example of how trials can lead to an extraordinary outcome. James faced numerous challenges, including persecution and martyrdom, yet he remained steadfast in his faith. His unwavering commitment to the Lord in the face of adversity is truly inspiring. By embracing a perspective of gratitude for the tragedies we have endured, we open ourselves up to a greater understanding of the purpose behind our sufferings. It is through these experiences that we develop resilience, strength, and compassion. We become better equipped to face future challenges and to offer support and encouragement to others who may be going through similar trials. In our daily lives, it is easy to dwell on our misfortunes and to become consumed by negativity. If we intentionally shift our focus towards gratitude, we can reframe our perspective and find purpose in even the most difficult circumstances.

Can we not shy away from the tragedies that befall us, but embrace them as opportunities for growth and transformation? Let us give thanks for the lessons learned, for the strength gained, and for the character developed in the face of adversity. By doing so, we can find joy in the midst of trials and inspire others with our unwavering faith.

5 If any of you lack wisdom, let him ask of God, that giveth to all men liberally, and upbraided not; and it shall be given him. 6 But let him ask in faith, nothing wavering. For he that wavered is like a wave of the sea driven with the wind and tossed. 7 For let not that man think that he shall receive any thing of the Lord. 8 A double minded man is unstable in all his ways.

Wow! James tells us to count it all joy when we fall into diverse temptations. That word *diverse* means *different.* Meaning the twelve tribes fell into different types of testing. Yes, the scriptures note that they were scattered abroad. The children of Israel in Judges 3 fell into different types of testing. **The fruit of the spirit is patience and joy, as you can see is a victory over tragedy.** Please do not miss this revelation. Having these two fruits of the Spirit coupled with the **Spirit of Wisdom** at work in you during your time of testing is a biblical assurance that you will receive from the Lord. It pleases Him to see us activating the fruit of the Spirit in our life. In fact, it is a major warfare key to aid you in your elevation.

When you are weighted with sin, grief, worry, doubt, confusion, dismay, depression, or any other negative weight, it prohibits you from being able to soar. Weights prohibit the believer from lifting their eyes unto the hill of The Lord from where their help comes from. How? Glad you asked, because weight takes the focus off Big G and puts it on little g. In other words, if you could tap into worship and begin to worship your way through your circumstance you can find rest. You, my friend, can find freedom, deliverance, which brings about healing to the believer. Jesus so eloquently puts it this way. His yoke is easy. I call this *"The Great Exchange."* You have tried everything else, now try Jesus! The thing with us humans is that we become accustomed to managing life's situations on our own. I remember losing my stepfather to a heinous murder at the hands of my baby brother, and I in my thirties did not know how to process all the emotions that came with a loss of that magnitude. I worked and drank the feelings of anger, sadness, and grief away. My choice of drink was red wine and a martini with amaretto in it. I just could not be alone with my thoughts. The grief was taking over me. When I did not work, I ate alone and when I was not eating, I was shopping, and when I was not shopping, I was drinking discreetly. You see, prior to that incident in 2012, I was not a drinker, but the enemy used grief to activate that vice in my family lineage.

Who could I really talk to? No one in my church could discern that I was not ok! My business demanded I have it together and be on point. My children needed me to at least be available when they needed me, but if I could be honest emotionally, I was unavailable. My husband needed me to be available when he needed me most. My body was there, but my mind was always somewhere else. Everyone had a need that required my healing and deliverance to be put cn hold. I mean, like most people did not even realize, I needed deliverance, and this essentially prolonged my elevation until my abrupt relocation to Georgia. What I love about Christianity through faith in Christ is: no tragedy can keep you bound. When there is a clear call of God on your life, and you have been chosen to be a vessel of impact. The Lord will move heaven and earth, I mean disrupt all your business and all the noise in your life to position you for spiritual elevation. Most of us, when we are making money and feeling accomplished in life, know what success feels and looks like. Take it all away and we are left to sit and stew in our thoughts. Well, as I previously said, you were never meant to go through the process alone. That is why it has taken me over 6 years to write 50 days of elevation. I am so glad that I did, but I had a lot of unpacking to do. It required a great deal of sifting, sorting, and purging of things physically and emotionally. Things that were tied to my identity as a business owner, which had nothing to do with where I was headed and what I was called to do in the kingdom of God.

When there is a clear call of God on your life, and you have been chosen to be a vessel of impact. The Lord will move heaven and earth, I mean disrupt all your business and all the noise in your life to position you for spiritual elevation.

Thoughts Of Virtue

THINK OF DIFFERENT TRIALS AND RENAME THEM JOY IN FAITH

_____

_____

_____

_____

_____

_____

_____

_____

_____

_____

_____

If any of you lack wisdom, let him ask of God, that giveth to all men liberally, and upbraided not; and it shall be given him. [6] *But let him ask in faith, nothing wavering. For he that wavered is like a wave of the sea driven with the wind and tossed.* [7] *For let not that man think that he shall receive any thing of the Lord.* [8] *A double minded man is unstable in all his ways.*

James 1:5-8

THE GREAT EXCHANGE

Welcome Day 12

Look at Matthew 11:27 for more clarity. *Matthew 11:27, All things are delivered unto me of my Father: and no man knoweth the Son, but the Father; neither knoweth any man the Father, save the Son, and he to whomsoever the Son will reveal him.[28] Come unto me, all ye that labor and are heavy laden, and I will give you rest.[29] Take my yoke upon you and learn of me; for I am meek and lowly in heart: and ye shall find rest unto your souls.[30] For my yoke is easy, and my burden is light.*

Ever feel like shouting? I am telling you, when you surrender yourself to worship and let the Holy Spirit take the lead, you will defeat that heaviness and sorrow weighing you down. Speaking of weight, that word also translates to "heavy" and "kabod". Carrying around past trauma and pain is like carrying unnecessary baggage, with no benefit or value. Here me, there is no gain in struggling through life without rest. When you cannot sleep because of tormenting thoughts, cry out for deliverance. The Lord wants to give you peace and sweet dreams. Make the decision to not let heaviness control you anymore. You are equipped with joy, patience, and wisdom, which holds the key to your breakthrough. It is time to break open every spiritual casket and grave that has held you captive. Do not forget to turn to Romans chapter 8, meditate on this chapter when the enemy tries to bring you down during your journey upwards towards your elevation. *Romans 8:1 There is therefore now no condemnation to those who are in Christ Jesus, who[a] do not walk according to the flesh, but according to the Spirit. ² For the law of the Spirit of life in Christ Jesus has made me free from the law of sin and death. ³ For what the law could not do in that it was weak through the flesh, God did by sending His own Son in the likeness of sinful flesh, on account of sin: He condemned sin in the flesh, ⁴ that the righteous requirement of the law might be fulfilled in us who do not walk according to the flesh but according to the Spirit. ⁵ For those who live according to the flesh set their minds on the things of the flesh, but those who live according to the Spirit, the things of the Spirit. ⁶ For to be [b]carnally minded is death, but to be spiritually minded is life and peace.*

⁷ Because the [c]carnal mind is enmity against God; for it is not subject to the law of God, nor indeed can be. ⁸ So then, those who are in the flesh cannot please God.

Let us decree this positive confession over your life today:

Today, I declare that my spirit is free from guilt, sin, and shame. I choose to walk in the spirit every day and overcome my flesh in moments of weakness. I'm beautiful, fearfully, and wonderfully made, and I shall fulfill the plan of God for my life through my spiritual elevation. Through Christ Jesus, I have victory over death of every kind. Hallelujah! All glory to God! I am no longer condemned or a victim of my past or its circumstances.

It is time to reclaim and elevate your life through the Spirit. Remember, Satan cannot touch your life in Christ, this is confirmed in scripture. Can you imagine being buried alive? That is how it feels to live with sin, guilt, and shame. It makes you lifeless and purposeless. Thank God for the gift of salvation. You are no longer weighed down by heavy spirits and burdens, for John 8:36 says, "If the Son sets you free, you will be free indeed." Remember, freedom through Christ is the greatest gift one can receive. Let us continue your 50 days of Elevation, and together, we will ascend to the Hill of The Lord– the high place. Think of all the things that have weighed you down and let the gift of freedom liberate you.

Thoughts Of Virtue

WHAT AREA IN YOUR LIFE CAN LIBERTY INHABIT?

_____

_____

_____

_____

_____

_____

_____

_____

_____

_____

_____

_____

_____

Now the Lord is that Spirit: and where the Spirit of the Lord is, there is liberty. [18] *But we all, with open face beholding as in a glass the glory of the Lord, are changed into the same image from glory to glory, even as by the Spirit of the Lord.*

2 Cor3:17-18

DEVELOP YOUR STRIDE

Welcome to Day 13

It is important to develop and understand your stride, as it defines who you are. There are three key components that can help prepare you for success. They were crucial for me, because when God elevated me, I was in the most comfortable yet uncomfortable season of my life. I did not understand what was happening and all the areas where I thought I had grown in my career were suddenly torn apart within just seven days. I found myself in the middle of nowhere, far away from the people I knew and loved. It felt like a small mansion in the wilderness. This phase of development was both familiar and unfamiliar, and there will be times in your life when God will allow you to be in what you consider your dream home, dream job, or married to your dream partner, only to realize that you are still in a state of discomfort. How is this possible, you may ask?

Let me guide you through what happened to me in October and November 2016. Over the span of just seven days, God allowed my physical home to be auctioned off. It was sold in March of that year, but we did not find out until October. Not to mention, I had moved my business to a new, bigger and better location nearby. Deep inside, I felt the pressure and hoped this was all just a bad dream, but it was not. I did not know who to confide in, and I eventually shared my struggles with a few trusted employees, giving them the option of keeping the business running. As I quickly found out, your dream is not their dream. My dream was a speed line to their next stop. As business owners we must remember that some people will only support what they can see. The walls were closing in on me, and I had to decide quickly. Little did I know that this was just the beginning of my spiritual elevation. It all started with a disruption. Can I offer you some encouragement? When God wants to develop you, He will disrupt what you hold closest to your heart. For me, I threw myself into work, as it was easier than facing my financial issues. Eventually, my carefully constructed life as a sweet young entrepreneur began to burst at the seams. In just a few months, the doors were closed, and the disruption to my spiritual eruption had begun.

Thoughts Of Virtue

WHAT DID GOD DISRUPT TO DEVELOP IN YOU?

_____

_____

_____

_____

_____

_____

_____

_____

_____

_____

_____

_____

For I know the plans I have for you, declares the LORD, plans for welfare and not for evil, to give you a future and a hope. Then you will call upon me and come and pray to me, and I will hear you. You will seek me and find me when you seek me with all your heart.

Jer 29:11-13

FINDING MY STRIDE

Welcome to Day 14

While reflecting on my disruption, about one year later I had an epiphany, that God had a completely different plan for my life. I became fully vested in this place of development discerning it needed my undivided attention, and it was then that I felt the calling of God, urging me to move forward. This marked the beginning of the Lord's hand in continuing to develop my spiritual life. Before this, constructing a message and fully understanding the Word was a struggle for me. However, I had a passion for reading and studying the Word of God. It was during this time, while living in a beautiful home in the wilderness of Conyers that I began to elevate. I remained connected to my home church in New Jersey and continued to pray with word of life wailing women again daily. I had been consecrated in 2005 as a prayer warrior for my church. Having the business and some personal transitions had previously caused me to fall away from my commitment between 2012-2016.

My hunger for the Lord grew even stronger and was noticed by my Intercessory prayer leader of twenty-two years, the late Pastor Joyce Huggins, who allowed me to take flight. She referred to a few of us as daughters. I affectionately called her Ma. Pastor Huggins encouraged, supported, and helped to cultivate the ministry flame within me, and so many others.

Pastor Huggins has completed prayer assignments all over the world. She is greatly missed.

Let me tell you a little about my experience. In 2017, I made a commitment to pray five days a week at 7:00 AM and start a 6:00 AM prayer group. Little did I know, this was just the beginning of my journey towards discovering spiritual elevation and revelation from God Through this dedicated time of prayer and seeking God's face, I began to experience a deeper connection with Christ and started to receive greater understanding and insight into the word of God. It took me being still with nothing to do for months. I had to allow the Lord to process me. Decompress even from my day-to-day routine. Fast forward to today, I see many people talking about elevation, but have not counted the cost. Unless you are ready to self-reflect, be incubated by yourself in the womb of life, uncomfortable until you discover the comforter (Holy-Spirit) must I go on? You are not elevating. Elevation is an internal soul work. It is an extraction of every superficial lie you ever told yourself about coping through life's hardships, letdowns, peaks, and valleys. Elevation is a discovery of your spiritual frequency that you might simply become a vessel of impact in this life. Elevation is learning how to harness the flame that you carry so that no matter what you encounter in this life you my friend stay lit. I digress.

Many seek the level of grace and anointing that their pastors or spiritual leaders carry but fail to understand the role of covenant relationships in this process.

Let me explain what I mean by covenant relationships. In the book of Habakkuk 2, the prophet speaks about how the vision has an appointed time and, though it may seem delayed, we must wait for it. In the same way, the harvest that has been placed within us also has an appointed time. I am reminded of the story of Elijah and Elisha, where Elijah served Elisha and in return, the man of God asked his servant what did he desire of him? Elisha requested a double portion. Elisha explained that he had requested a hard thing, but if he would be with him when he was taken up, then he would receive a double portion of his spirit. When Elijah was taken up in a whirlwind, his mantle fell and Elisha picked it up, and I should say it was at that time his ministry began.

Unfortunately, in this generation of believers, we have seen a rise in the desire for quick results and instant gratification. Thanks to social media and other platforms, we have been exposed to spiritual teachings and experiences that make it seem like we can achieve the same level of power and anointing overnight, but this is simply not true.

We must understand that *elevation is a process*, and it requires a deep commitment to God and a covenant relationship with Him. Just as a seed takes time to grow into a fruitful plant, our spiritual growth and elevation take time and effort. We cannot skip steps or bypass the process. I beseech you, during this elevation, focus on building a strong and committed relationship with God. May we not be fooled by the shiny external appearance of other people's social display of their lives, because all that glitters ain't gold. Spiritual elevation without *incubation, consecration, and revelation will eventually lead to procrastination.* These are the three keys needed to unlock your spiritual elevation. They serve as proof that truly the Lord is with you. Let us trust in God's timing and continue to seek Him diligently.

Finally, I want to leave you with the words of Habakkuk 2:2, where the prophet says, "Write the vision and make it plain on tablets, that he may run who reads it." Let us take the time to write down our aspirations and desires during this time of spiritual elevation, and most importantly, let us commit them to God in prayer. May we all continue to walk in the process of elevation with joy and patience, knowing that God is in control and His timing is perfect. We must *remember that elevation requires disruption. Development requires submission and subscription. You must subscribe to the process.* Hallelujah! Now that's revelation. We pay for all kinds of subscriptions, waste money on many that we rarely use, and companies do not monitor our use, but our monthly fee serves as a metric of satisfaction. Think of ways that you can subscribe to developing your life as a believer.

Spiritual elevation without incubation, consecration, and revelation will eventually lead to procrastination.

Thoughts Of Virtue

CAN YOU SUBSCRIBE TO BE DEVELOPED IN CHRIST?

_____

_____

_____

_____

_____

_____

_____

_____

_____

_____

_____

I therefore, the prisoner of the Lord, beseech you that ye walk worthy of the vocation wherewith ye are called,[2] With all lowliness and meekness, with longsuffering, forbearing one another in love;[3] Endeavoring to keep the unity of the Spirit in the bond of peace.

Ephesians 4:11

EMOTIONAL STRIDE

Welcome to day 15 of our 50 days of elevation.

As we continue to focus on elevating our spiritual walk, today we will dive into the concept of "harnessing your emotional stride." This term may be unfamiliar to some, so let me break it down and see how it relates to your elevation.

According to the dictionary, stride means to walk with long, decisive steps in a specified direction. It can also mean to cross an obstacle with one long step. What does this have to do with our emotions? Well, it turns out that our emotions have a direct impact on our stride and on how we move forward in life.

Think about it: what we say, think, feel and, ultimately, how we move are all affected and connected to our emotional state. When we experience shifts in our emotions, it can either bring us up and help us excel or bring us down and cause us to fail. It is like a steering wheel for our actions and behaviors.

One powerful influence on our emotions is sound. We have all experienced how certain songs can make us feel happy, sad, or even pumped up. This is because sound has the ability to activate our brain waves associated with emotional processing. Just think about how classical music can have a calming effect on babies, or how a certain song can make us want to dance, immediately you begin to bob your head or pat your feet. The power of sound is undeniable.

Stay with me as we explore the context of worship?

As believers, we know that worship is a significant part of our Christianity experience. There is often an arguable stigma attached to the worship encounter. Many come to church for the "praise and worship" experience, and if it does not meet their expectations, they are out or just in time for the sermon. This trend reveals a shallow understanding of worship and shows how our emotions can be manipulated by external factors. We must remember that true worship goes beyond just feeling good or getting goosebumps. It is a heartfelt expression of our love and gratitude towards God. As believers, we can't be, so personality focused that we are not Christ driven.

During our elevation, we may encounter challenges and obstacles that come to shake our emotional stability. This means we are in the perfect place of confrontation. Take advantage in this moment to confront what comes up out of your heart and know that this time you are not doing it alone. You have the help of the Holy Spirit and an entire support group of intercessors praying for you to move to your next place in Christ. We must continue to develop our sound through prayer, fasting and meditation, and forgive those who hurt us, even ourselves, if we did not handle a situation gracefully. We are still a work in progress, constantly striving to embody the heart of Christ. As we learn to harness our emotions and let the Holy Spirit guide us, we can walk through any obstacle with confidence and grace.

In conclusion, let us not be driven by our emotions, but by the obedience of Christ Jesus. We must bring every thought, driven by emotions, into captivity, and focus on the abundance of our hearts. Remember, the heavens know and obey our sound, so let us make sure it is aligned with God's will.

On this 15th day of elevation, continue to strive towards a deeper understanding and control of our emotions. Let us continue to develop our emotional stride and move confidently along the course The Lord has set for us. We are not our feelings; we are children of God, walking in His love and grace. Keep elevating!

Thoughts Of Virtue

DO THE HEAVENS KNOW YOUR SOUND?

_____

_____

_____

_____

_____

_____

_____

_____

_____

_____

_____

_____

It shall be when you hear the sound of marching in the tops of the balsam trees, then you shall go out to battle, for God will have gone out before you to strike the army of the Philistines."

1Chron 14:15

I AM NOT MY FEELINGS

Welcome to Day 16 of our 50 days of elevation.

Can you believe we are already over two weeks into this? Time truly flies when we are growing in our faith, huh? Speaking of growth, today's topic is one that I am sure many of us struggle with – feelings. I coined it from day 15.

We have all been there. Those times when our emotions decide to take over and steer us down a dark and treacherous path. It is like a rabbit hole with no exit, and before we know it, we are completely consumed.

Here is the thing, as believers, we have a weapon to combat these tricky feelings, prayer. Yes, that is right. During these 50 days, I urge you to make a conscious effort to spend time in early morning prayer. Preferably 5a.m. I know, I know. Some of you are not morning people (raises hand guiltily), but trust me, it will be worth it.

You see, our feelings often dictate our actions, especially when it comes to relationships. We can easily write someone off because we do not "feel" a certain way about them, without even giving them a chance.

Let's turn the focus back to ourselves. When we are going through a tough trial, we let our feelings take the wheel, and it is not always pretty.

We do not feel like getting out of bed, going to church, or even getting dressed. Our circumstances have consumed our thoughts, and we are now being led by our feelings, rather than by our spirit. The Bible tells us to be led by the Spirit, not our emotions. If I can be honest, our feelings can be fickle and unreliable at times.

What can we do to combat this trap of feelings? First off, let us remember that we are nothing without Christ. We need His strength and guidance to navigate through life's trials. Second, we need to decree the word of God over ourselves. Remember, there is no condemnation for those in Christ (Romans 8:1). Speak this truth over yourself every day.

Moreover, let us ask for the gift of discernment, so we can recognize when our emotions are trying to take over and prejudge a person or situation in our flesh. Finally, let us strive to be like Jesus, who was led by the spirit in every situation. The Bible gives us so many verses about being led by the spirit, such as Galatians 5:16 and Romans 8:14. Let's meditate on these verses and make it a daily practice to check our actions and thoughts, so we can be sure we're following the leading of the spirit, not our feelings.

In conclusion, my dear friend, let us remember that we are equipped to face any battle that comes our way. We have the word of God to guide us, and the spirit of God to lead us.

Today we must get out of our feelings, into the word, and find our tools and weapons to fight any internal or external warfare that comes our way. As always, let us continue to lift each other up and encourage one another in our journey to becoming overcomers through Christ. Stay strong, stay faithful, and let us keep elevating!

Elevation – Transformation = Stagnation

Thoughts Of Virtue

WHEN YOU FEEL_____YOU SAY OR DO _____?

_____

_____

_____

_____

_____

_____

_____

_____

_____

_____

_____

_____

"You have heard that it was said, 'Eye for eye, and tooth for tooth.'[a] 39 But I tell you, do not resist an evil person. If anyone slaps you on the right cheek, turn to them the other cheek also. 40 And if anyone wants to sue you and take your shirt, hand over your coat as well.

Matt5:38-40

SPIRITUAL STRIDE

Welcome back to day 17 of the 50 days of elevation.

Today we will explore the book of 3 John. Look at verse two. He is talking directly to you, reminding you that you are beloved and that he prays for your success and prosperity in every aspect of your life. Take a moment to let that sink in. Allow these words to wash over you. *You are beloved and you are meant to succeed and prosper in life, even as your soul prospers.*

In a more common way that scripture may read, beloved above all things I wish that you would prosper even as your soul prospers. That means there is absolutely nothing more important to the Lord Jesus than your spiritual, and emotional well-being. As John prays for you to prosper spiritually, let us remember that your soul and spiritual well-being are directly linked to your physical health and success. Prosperity is not just about money or material possessions; it is about flourishing in all areas of your life.

Now take a closer look at the word "prosper". It is an action word, meaning it requires movement and action. To prosper is to have a fruitful and successful journey, physically and spiritually. It means to grow and become strong and healthy.

The dictionary even defines it as "to be successful". And here is the key: your thoughts play a crucial role in your prosperity.

The book of Philippians reminds us, what we meditate on the most will determine the course of our lives. If we constantly think about defeat and being overwhelmed, then that is what we will attract and become. Our minds must be renewed, and we must break free from any negative programming that may be holding us back.

In the book of Psalms 37:4, we are reminded to rejoice and take pleasure in the Lord always. *Delight yourself in Him and He will give you the desires of your heart.* When we shift our thoughts and focus on God, we align ourselves with His plan for our lives. Our success and prosperity are directly tied to our relationship with Him.

Today, let us awaken our spiritual stride and walk in the truth of God's eternal word. Today choose to delight in the Lord and trust in His plan for our lives. As we continue to elevate, remember that you are beloved, and you are meant to succeed and prosper in every way. Amen.

Elevation – Transformation = Stagnation

Thoughts Of Virtue

WHAT STEPS CAN YOU TAKE TO COMAND YOUR SOUL TO
PROSPER?

_____

_____

_____

_____

_____

_____

_____

_____

_____

_____

_____

_____

_____

If then you have been raised with Christ, seek the things that are above, where Christ is, seated at the right hand of God. ² Set your minds on things that are above, not on things that are on earth.

Col 3:4

ANXIOUS FOR WHAT?

To God be the Glory, it is Day 18 of 50 days of elevation, and you are still going strong.

There is no need to be anxious or worried about anything. I mean it, nothing. Don't you know that in every circumstance and situation, you have a secret weapon? Allow me to expound on your weapons' prayer and petition. Petition, that is when you open your mouth and make a decree. It is like putting in your order with God. What is your expectation? What are you asking for? Oh, I love this definition of petition: a formal written request, usually signed by many, appealing to authority for a particular cause.

Stay with me, I am teaching right now. There is a difference between prayer and petition. Your prayer is not the same as your petition. You must know how to pray. Philippians 4 says to make your request known to God. Your petition is your appeal to the one who is in authority. It is your request for God to attend to your specific need. The bible says to make your request known to God in other words be specific in your asking.

Philippians 4:6-8 says, do not be anxious or worried about anything. Instead, pray and make your request known to God, with thanksgiving. Did you catch that? *Prayer, petition, and thanksgiving are the keys*. When you do those three things, you must be reassured in your heart with His peace that it is done. This peace transcends all understanding and stands guard over your heart and mind.

Finally, believe this: whatever is true, honorable, right, pure, lovely, admirable, excellent, and worthy of praise, think about these things. You know what, my friend? These things can only be confirmed by God's word. Take a moment to meditate on this. Let it sink in and guide your thoughts and remember, you have peace, and it is all yours.

Today, get up and go out there and let your light shine today. Be gracious, unselfish, merciful, patient, and tolerant, and when you encounter challenges, remember the power of prayer and petition. Be specific about your requests and give thanks. Above all, think about these admirable, excellent, and praiseworthy things. Go ahead, elevate today. You got this!

Thoughts Of Virtue

HOW HAS ANXIETY ROBBED YOU OF YOUR PEACE?

_____
_____
_____
_____
_____
_____
_____
_____
_____
_____
_____
_____
_____
_____
_____

Brethren, I count not myself to have apprehended: but this one thing I do, forgetting those things which are behind, and reaching forth unto those things which are before,[14] I press toward the mark for the prize of the high calling of God in Christ Jesus.

Phil 3:13

THE BATTLE IS THE LORDS

WELCOME TO DAY 19

Are you ready to embark on the 19th day of your 50-day journey to elevation? The Lord is raising up fearless warriors for the Kingdom of God, you have been fighting battles and facing trials. The enemy knows of your strength and has been trying to get to you in any way possible, through your loved ones, betrayal, and even doubts.

Here the Good News! It is time for you to walk under an open heaven and experience heavenly encounters like never before. How amazing does that sound? The Lord has spoken, and He has a plan for you. Do not lose heart, instead, focus on seeking Him through fasting and prayer. Trust in His plan and continue to discipline yourself for the remaining days.

I know it may be tempting to look for big, flashy signs of God's presence, but the Lord says to simply seek Him and trust that His hand is guiding you. The Lord Jesus will bring you through this profound moment with strength, revelation, and heavenly breakthrough. Do not allow doubt of any kind to hold you back. Instead, have faith and believe in the Lord's promises.

As you continue to press towards your elevation, know that you have heavenly approval. Your faith and obedience will not go unnoticed by the most- high God. I believe in you and, most importantly, The Lord Jesus believes in you. He has a plan for your life, and it is full of blessings, provision, and miracles.

The Lord is your defender, as He was for David, Joshua, and Debra. Cooperate with Christ and follow His plan for your life. Know that He is fighting your battles and protecting you. Do not doubt the power of the Lord and the plans He has for your life. He wants nothing but the best for you because you are His beloved child.

At times, we struggle to see ourselves the way God sees us. Remember, you are created in His image, and He sees you as beautiful, strong, and full of power. He is filling your mind with His heavenly thoughts, waking you up in the early hours of the morning to start your day. The Lord desires to fill you with His truth, His word, and His strength. Let go of any thoughts that would try to grip you and cause you to be stagnate today. Remember that you too can be a warrior for the Kingdom of God. Put on your armor, stand strong, and claim the victory that is already yours.

Thoughts Of Virtue

WHAT ARE SOME BATTLES YOU NEED THE LORD TO FIGHT?

_____

_____

_____

_____

_____

_____

_____

_____

_____

_____

_____

_____

_____

_____

_____

Jesus saith unto him, I am the way, the truth, and the life: no man cometh unto the Father, but by me.

John14:6

DIMENSIONLESS

Welcome back to Day 20 of 50 Days of Elevation.

I am excited to dive deeper into the topic of the power within us - the Ruach Hakodesh, or the Holy Spirit.

As mentioned before, The Holy Spirit is the driving force, The Spirit of God constantly at work within us. Corinthians 3:16 says, *do you not know that you are a temple of God and that the Spirit of God dwells in you?* It is what makes us limitless, and yet, many of us often limit ourselves to the physical world and forget about the power within us.

Let me give you a simple physics lesson. According to mass and physics, mass is a measurement of matter in an object, with no defined dimension. According to the famous equation $E=mc^2$, energy equals mass multiplied by the speed of light squared. Simply put, we have the potential to be dimensionless beings, moving at the speed of light, thanks to the spirit of God within us.

Think about it - when we pray in the spirit, there are no limitations in prayer. The Father will not stop you from seeking Him day and night. This is why the word tells us to pray without ceasing. We have the potential to tap into higher dimensions and operate at the speed of light. Ask yourself, why do we often keep our mouths closed and limit ourselves to a multidimensional world?

For example. Imagine yourself as E=MC², a body full of energy, one who can operate at the speed of light. Let me help you. Now imagine The Father creating you to experience him in other dimensions through prayer.

Let me share an experience I had while praying with a friend of mine. The Holy Spirit gave me a word of knowledge, addressing the air traffic controllers in the spiritual realm, which were causing spiritual delays in our life. Much like in the book of Daniel chapter ten, where Gabriel the angel assigned to answer the prayer of Daniel is held up by the prince of Persia, Archangel Michael steps in and clear the way for Gabriel to now fulfill his assignment for Daniel who has been fasting for a period of 21 days.

In the same way an unseen traffic jam or a prince over the region in which you are in can cause delays in your physical life. There can be congestion in the spiritual realm, holding up your prayer and progress to overcome a situation in a specific territory. Through the power of the Holy Spirit within us and prayer, we have the authority to command the air traffic controllers to clear the way.

 I urge you to tap into this multidimensional blessing that God has given us. Our advantage is, we have the Ruach, the spirit of the true and living God inside us. We have the power to overcome any obstacle or limitations through consistent covenant prayer and fasting. As a believer you cannot be afraid to operate at the speed of light because you are salt and light. Look at Matthew 5:13. *You are the salt of the earth; but if the salt has lost its taste (purpose), how can it be made salty? It is no longer good for anything, but to be thrown out and walked on by people [when the walkways are wet and slippery].*

[14] *"You are the light of [Christ to] the world. A city set on a hill cannot be hidden;* [15] *nor does anyone light a lamp and put it under a basket, but on a lampstand, and it gives light to all who are in the house.* [16] *Let your light shine before men in such a way that they may see your good deeds and moral excellence, and [recognize and honor and] glorify your Father who is in heaven.*

Remember, you are $E=MC^2$, with the potential to operate beyond the limits of this world. Every prince set over the region in which The Lord has assigned you must bow to the power of consistent prayer. Know that there are angels assigned to aid you here on the earth that the Father would be glorified. Elevate more!

Thoughts Of Virtue

HOW HAVE YOU LIMITED YOURSELF IN PRAYER?

_____

_____

_____

_____

_____

_____

_____

_____

_____

_____

_____

_____

_____

_____

_____

[3] *And he put forth the form of a hand, and took me by a lock of my head; and the spirit lifted me up between the earth and the heaven, and brought me in the visions of God to Jerusalem,*

Ezek 8

THE BLESSING OF 29

Welcome to Day 21 of our 50-day journey towards elevation.

Today is a pivotal moment. You may be curious about what sets today apart from the rest. My friend, the fact that we still have 29 days left on this journey is a clear indication that we are in alignment to receive divine blessings. Let us take a moment to contemplate the significance of the number 29. This number holds significant meaning in the scriptures; for example, the renowned King Hezekiah ruled over Judah for 29 years, and during the final stages of His ministry, Jesus fed 5000 people in 29 AD. Shortly after, He also performed another incredible miracle in Galilee by feeding 4000 more, as recorded in the scriptures. As I write to you today, I urge you to reflect deeply on how you will use your remaining 29 days.

Maybe it's been a rocky start and you have not been able to get calibrated with your elevation. If that is the case don't sink in defeat. Trust me those who have completed this regimen with me know how we had days where we just simply deflated. I encourage you to zoom in on what you desire your life to look like. Knowing and understanding the prophetic timeline of your life is essential to you not missing your elevation. I urge you to be sensitive to how things happen to you and what month it happened. These are patterns and cycles. Cycles are important because they can last a period of seven years. Which means also that cycles can be broken whether good, bad, self-inflicted, or inflicted unknowingly on you. Patterns on the other hand, can be tied to how you function in your daily life. Think of your morning routine, what it consists of and how it affects your day when it is broken, or out of alignment. Now apply the same thought principle to understanding your personal elevation. In conclusion slowing down to assess your life's cycles and patterns is essential to your personal elevation in every area of your life.

May this message today ignite a sense of self-awareness within you, and may you use this moment to pivot spiritually, physically, and emotionally from unhealthy patterns and cycles that no longer serve you.

Elevation – Transformation = Stagnation

Thoughts Of Virtue

WHAT PATTERNS AND CYCLES DO YOU NEED TO BREAK TO ELEVATE?

_____

_____

_____

_____

_____

_____

_____

_____

_____

_____

_____

_____

[25] Then he answered, "I do not know whether He is a sinner [separated from God]; but one thing I do know, that though I was blind, now I see.

John9:25

A SIMPLE PRAYER

Welcome to Day 22.

As people, we often face challenges and trials in our daily lives. It is easy to get caught up in our own problems and forget to offer even a simple prayer for guidance and strength. Sometimes, all it takes is a few words spoken in faith to bring about a powerful change. Today, I want to share with you a simple prayer - a prayer that has the power to bring peace, healing, and blessings into your life. It is a prayer that has been passed down for generations, rooted in the promises of Christ Jesus.

"Father, I am grateful for the fire you have placed on this altar. I surrender myself completely to you, knowing that you are Jehovah-Rapha, our Healer. Thank you for healing us from all our diseases."

The first part of this prayer acknowledges that God is our provider and protector. It reminds us He has the power to heal us from any physical or emotional ailments we may be facing. As we surrender ourselves to His will, we can trust that He will take care of us.

"You have the power and anointing to touch and release us from any burdens and yokes that the enemy tries to put on me."

The next part of this prayer recognizes that there is an enemy who seeks to bring us down and hinder our growth. We have a powerful savior on our side who breaks every chain and sets us free. By declaring these words, we are claiming victory over the schemes of the enemy.

"I thank you for touching me and for your Word, which will destroy every scheme of the enemy."

We must never underestimate the power of God's Word. It is a mighty weapon against the enemy's lies, discomfort, and confusion. By meditating on His promises and speaking His truth, we can overcome any obstacle that comes our way.

"Your Word will go forth and destroy every lie, discomfort, and confusion."

God's promises are sure and His plans for us are good. As we continue to trust in His promises, He will expand our territories and give us an extended range. He will open doors and provide opportunities that we never thought possible.

"I believe in your promises, your ministry, your vision, and everything you have spoken over me. I thank you for expanding my territory and giving me an extended range."

Remember it is not only about our personal growth and success. This prayer also reminds us to be grateful for the people God has brought into our lives. These individuals play a vital role in our journey, and we must never take them for granted.

"I TRUST IN YOUR LOVING KINDNESS TO DRAW OTHERS TO THIS MINISTRY AND TO HELP US LOVE AND SUPPORT ONE ANOTHER."

God's love is unfailing, and it flows through the hearts of the people He brings into our lives. Let us be grateful for their presence and the love they show us.

"Thank you for the hearts of the amazing people you have brought or are bringing into my life. Thank you for the sweet, unfailing love that flows from you through them."

As we end this prayer, let us remember that God's loving kindness will always be upon us. It is through His love that we can reach out to others and draw them closer to Him.

"May your loving kindness always be upon me and draw others to you. In Jesus Christ's name, Amen."

I encourage you to speak this simple prayer every day and experience the power of God's promises in your life.

Thoughts Of Virtue

THERE'S A BLESSING IN CONFESSION

_____

_____

_____

_____

_____

_____

_____

_____

_____

_____

_____

_____

_____

_____

[17] *So then faith cometh by hearing, and hearing by the word of God.*
Rom 10:17

HEAVEN ON EARTH

As we approach day 23 of our 50 days of elevation, it is important to reflect on the purpose behind our mission.

Our main goal should be to actively work towards improving and enforcing the principles of heaven on earth. I believe that The Lord Jesus has commanded us to do so, as his followers and representatives. Let's look at what Jesus has to say in John 14:12. *I assure you and most solemnly say to you, anyone who believes in Me [as Savior] will also do the things that I do; and he will do even greater things than these [in extent and outreach], because I am going to the Father. 13 And I will do whatever you ask [in My name as My representative], this I will do, so that the Father may be glorified and celebrated in the Son. 14 If you ask Me anything in My name [as My representative], I will do it.*

John is a key to us understanding the heavenly access we have been given through Christ. Often, we tend to accept sickness, illness, struggles, and unhealthy relationships as the norm in our lives, when clearly these are not attributes of the authority we have been given through Christ. We may pray for healing and deliverance, but how do we maintain our healing and deliverance once we have received it? Heaven on earth is not some foreign concept or cliché, it is heaven abiding in you always. To harness spiritual health, you must maintain your spiritual environment. Think of things that may be cluttering your heart, mind, or even your home. What space do you spend the most time in? Have you dedicated a place to pray, study the word, or simply have that time of devotion with The Lord Jesus. I'm reminded of a homeowner's association that has someone to monitor the community, making sure that the new homes remain beautiful and hold their value. We too have a community and environment to maintain after receiving Christ or breakthrough. There can be spiritual debris scattered on our grounds, but it cannot grow within the community of our hearts and mind. We must not forget that our body is a temple. How we demonstrate what we say we believe is correlated through our sonship, and willingness to partner with the Holy Spirit.

My prayer is that there is a reformation happening in you now! I believe that 50 days of elevation is a personal call to reformation. It will take having consistent faith to challenge the systems that have been holding you back and limiting your spiritual growth. There is no greater moment than now, to step out in faith and trust that the Holy Spirit will guide you in dismantling every system that devalues who you were created to be in Christ.

Thoughts Of Virtue

WHAT PERAMITERS CAN YOU PUT IN PLACE TO MAINTAIN
YOUR SPIRITUAL VALUE?

_____

_____

_____

_____

_____

_____

_____

_____

_____

_____

_____

_____

_____

_____

_____

_____

"Don't give holy things to depraved men. Do not give pearls to swine! They will trample the pearls and turn and attack you.

Matt 7:6

THE THIEF AND YOUR TREASURE

Welcome to Day 24

You should certainly be experiencing a greater since of clarity and spiritual elevation. Especially if you have truly been doing the work. Let us get into an insurable topic, *The thief, and your treasure.* The thief understands the value of what is in your house, even if you do not. You may not know what you are incubating, or what you are housing. The thief understands this concept and knows that if they can break in and steal from you, they will reap great rewards. I want to remind you that a true thief does not target material possessions. I do not mean to criticize those who have stolen in the past, but they do not understand the true value that Jesus spoke of. In most cases, the place they are breaking into is not worth the effort because the true value lies in your relationship with Christ Jesus. You may not realize this until something damages it, like an alarm going off too late. Sometimes, it is too late to do anything about it. Before you know it, you have lost all kinds of things-jewelry, material possessions, and most importantly, your peace of mind. How can you, as a believer, be specifically targeted by a thief? I believe that there is a reward for those who complete their assignment and often, this reward is dependent on the type of demonic forces that fight against you. These can come in many forms, such as witches, warlocks, or disembodied spirits that seek to rob us of our joy, our futures, and our overall well-being. Their mission is to create problems in our lives that ultimately result in death. These wicked attacks can manifest in our health, our relationships, and even our children or those who may be close to us. It is crucial to recognize these attacks and seek help to fight against them with the Lord's help. We must not allow these thieves to continue robbing us and preventing us from experiencing a high-quality life. Let us be vigilant and protect ourselves from demonic thieves who seek to harm us and may the Holy Spirit guide us every step of the way.

Please look at Matthew chapter 6:19, It discusses the importance of not accumulating earthly possessions. In verses 6 and 19, we are reminded to thank the Lord for His blessings. Here, it is stated *that we should not store treasure on Earth, as they are susceptible to damage and theft. Instead, we should focus on storing treasures in heaven, where they are safe from destruction and theft. This passage brings to mind the scripture in verse 21, which states that our desires are rooted in our treasured possessions.* Thus, it is vital to examine what we center our lives around, as those are the things targeted by the enemy. The Amplified Bible states we should not value material possessions, but rather focus on heavenly treasures, as that is where our true desires lie. We must ask ourselves, what do we give the most attention to? That is what the thief is after. Let that marinate for a moment.

In conclusion, our desires and thoughts are what the thief is after and what we value is what the robber wants. It is important to note that Jesus has paid the ransom for our souls, so the robbers and thieves no longer have a legal right to steal our joy, peace, or any other asset of value apart of our now and future inheritances. As stated in the book of Mark 10:45 and 1 Peter 1, God paid a ransom for our salvation through the precious life and blood of Jesus Christ, allowing us to put our trust and hope in Him alone. This means that we can now have genuine love for others, as our souls have been cleansed from selfishness and hatred when we trust in Christ to save us. Therefore, let us treasure heavenly things and remember that Jesus has paid the ultimate ransom for us.

The thief may understand the value of what is in your house, even if you do not.

Thoughts Of Virtue

WHAT DO YOU VALUE THE MOST? IT WILL REQUIRE MUCH
PRAYER.

_____

_____

_____

_____

_____

_____

_____

_____

_____

_____

_____

_____

*Do not store up for yourselves [material] treasures on earth, where
moth and rust destroy, and where thieves break in and steal*

Matt 6:19

MY HEART IS A TABERNACLE

Welcome to Day 25

The angels are patiently awaiting to fulfill the Father's will for mankind, especially for us who were created in His image. They desire to reaffirm and reinforce His word on earth. The Bible promises that His word will not return to Him unfulfilled, but rather will accomplish all it was intended to do. Therefore, it is up to us to speak God's word so that its full impact is accomplished in the area in which we have sent it. We can trust in the power of God's word, supported by the entirety of heaven, including the multitude of angels waiting eagerly to carry out His plans.

Today, I declare the confidence and victory we have in the word of God, and nothing can stand against it. We will confidently speak and establish the word of The Lord, knowing that it draws us into His presence. The Holy Spirit described this to me as The Prestige of Heaven. What are some things that you have dreamed of doing but for one reason or another, you stopped believing? I want you to begin declaring the word of God over these situations and watch eagerly like Habakkuk on your watch tower to see what The Lord will have you do. Write them as you begin to reflect. I love what the psalmist says in *119:9. How can a young man keep his way pure?*

By keeping watch [on himself] according to Your word [conforming his life to Your precepts].10 With all my heart I have sought You, [inquiring of You and longing for You];Do not let me wander from Your commandments [neither through ignorance nor by willful disobedience].11 Your word I have treasured and stored in my heart, That I may not sin against You. 12 Blessed and reverently praised are You, O Lord; Teach me Your statutes.

What a way to flex your heart muscle towards God! Who said you could not question God? Here you find the psalmist asking the Father to keep him in all his ways so that his actions would remain pure. I think of how every generation is exposed to a greater level of knowledge, some good and some that can completely corrupt your destiny. When we find ourselves being challenged as believers to live a life of purty it can seem obscure, meaning none of us really gets it all right. Through meditating on the word, we can come to a deeper place of fellowship that helps us to maintain our salvation (victory) in Christ as our hearts are transformed into a tabernacle.

Thoughts Of Virtue

LORD BUILD MY HEART TO SEE YOUR GLORY

_____

_____

_____

_____

_____

_____

_____

_____

_____

_____

_____

_____

I will climb up to my watchtower and stand at my guard post.
There I will wait to see what the Lord says the Lord.

Habbakuk2:1

THE PRESTIGE OF HEAVEN

Welcome to Day 26

The Holy Spirit told us that we would walk in the prestige of heaven on this day. Father, I declare that even after these 50 days, the prestige of heaven is still at work. That word is still alive, and we will continue to walk in the glory of God. When people look at us, they will see the manifestation of the blood of Jesus and the victory we have in Him. We will be living examples of working and walking in His word, and our lives will reflect the Kingdom produced by believers all over the earth. Thank you, Lord, for allowing us to grow and demonstrate Kingdom business in this earthly realm. The more you talk and pray about the Kingdom, the more God fills me with His agenda. I am not interested in discussing anything that is not on His heart and mind. We were sent to replicate Heaven's Kingdom on earth, and it is only through inquiring and seeking His will that our lives will truly reflect. It is imperative that you remember. I am a Kingdom producer, and I will always operate from a Kingdom perspective, bringing heaven's agenda to this earthly realm. Thank you, Jesus, for your blessings. Hallelujah!

Hey, this is a great spot for you to praise the Lord! Do not sit on that, let me help you, do not sleep on that either. Instead, ask God to fill you with His Kingdom agenda. That is all I have been praying for since I left Nashville in 2022. God has been speaking to me about His Kingdom even before I went there. He showed me that any business or task that does not align with His Kingdom will not be successful. I am at a point in my life where I only want to do what aligns with His Kingdom. Trust me, if it isn't the King's decree, it is a waste of time. Hear me out friends, whatever the King's decree is for your life, He will support it. Just look at Nehemiah's story. When he heard about the destruction of Jerusalem, he sat down, wept, and fasted. He prayed to God for guidance and pleaded for His mercy. When something heavy hits you, follow Nehemiah's example. Shed some tears, fast, and pray to the God of heaven. He keeps His promises and is merciful to those who love Him and follow His commandments. Let Him hear you and see your faith.

Nehemiah 1:1 In December of the twentieth year of the reign of King Artaxerxes of Persia,[a] when I was at the palace at Shushan, 2 one of my fellow Jews named Hanani came to visit me with some men who had arrived from Judah. I took the opportunity to inquire about how things were going in Jerusalem.

Upon hearing this, he was moved to tears and mourned for several days. He fasted and prayed before the God of heaven, acknowledging that when a heavy burden befalls us, we must also have a plan in place. Just like Nehemiah, who sat and mourned, fasting and beseeching God to hear his prayer day and night. He pleaded for the children of Israel, confessing their sins and asking for forgiveness. Nehemiah understood the importance of interceding, standing in the gap for his people, even acknowledging the transgressions of his own family. He was determined to break the curse and seek repentance for himself and his family lineage. Will you do the same?

Thoughts Of Virtue

WHAT DOES YOUR KINGDOM POSTURE RESEMBLE?

_____

_____

_____

_____

_____

_____

_____

_____

_____

_____

_____

_____

_____

_____

But now I tell them, "You know full well the tragedy of our city; it lies in ruins and its gates are burned. Let us rebuild the wall of Jerusalem and rid ourselves of this disgrace!"

Neh2:17

THE WORD HIDDEN IN YOUR HEART IS YOUR SWORD

Welcome to Day 27

It is difficult to say that you are a believer in Christ and not produce any real evidence of your conversion. I have found in my walk with Christ spanning over almost 30 years. Depending on what my heart posture was, that is what I produced. Until one day, I began to hear the word of God in my early twenties. I am telling you, I had to dig through the debris of life lodged in my soul. (I refer to this method in earlier chapters called sifting). Remember Hebrews 4:12 says Psalm 24

1 The earth is the Lord's, and all that therein is the world and they that dwell therein.

2 For he hath founded it upon the [a]seas; and established it upon the floods.

3 Who shall ascend into the mountain of the Lord? and who shall stand in his holy place?

4 Even he that hath innocent hands, and a pure heart, which hath not lifted his mind unto vanity, nor sworn deceitfully.

5 He shall receive a blessing from the Lord, and righteousness from the God of his salvation.

6 This is the [b]generation of them that seek him, of them that seek thy face, this is Jacob. Selah.

7 [c]Lift up your heads ye gates, and be ye lifted up ye everlasting doors, and the King of glory shall come in.

8 Who is this King of glory? the Lord, strong and mighty, even the Lord mighty in battle.

9 Lift up your heads, ye gates, and lift up yourselves ye everlasting doors, and the King of glory shall come in.

10 Who is this King of glory? the Lord of hosts, he is the King of glory. Selah. the word of God is quick, and powerful, and sharper than any two-edged sword, piercing even to the dividing asunder of soul and spirit, and of the joints and marrow, and is a discerner of the thoughts and intents of the heart. The word of God is sharper than any two-edged sword, so it was designed to cut coming and going. What I mean is no matter where you find yourself in life, if you are hearing the word and adhering to it, transformation is bound to take its course. You cannot and will not remain the same. You must produce what you have hidden in your heart. Make up in your mind and heart today that you will begin to produce from the kingdom to the earth. Essentially, you have switched your coordinates. You are no longer operating as a commoner, but more like royalty. When you understand your royal inheritance, you do not think about where you are going to eat or live. It was already given to you.

What? Yes, my friend, as a King's kid you are born into prestige. You are born into an automatic inheritance; you are born to defend the crown if that makes sense. Your very life and every decision you make reflects the crown. Oh, my goodness that revelation. As believers, we have a duty to defend the word of God. Anything in our lives that does not align with the king's decree concerning who we are and who we were created to be in this life (Your Spiritual Identity) must be challenged. Check Your heart, assess everything around you and make sure it is a product of the Kingdom of Heaven and what you should be producing. In other words, examine your fruit. For example, if you had an orange grove or apple orchard, you are not taking your harvest to the market and it's a bad batch, you will examine the harvest to make sure it's profitable for that season. Likewise concerning your spiritual fruit, we must examine what we are producing seasonally or daily to ensure a profitable harvest.

Thoughts Of Virtue

WHAT ARE YOU PRODUCING?

_____

_____

_____

_____

_____

_____

_____

_____

_____

_____

_____

_____

_____

_____

Jesus answers them, "It is not the healthy who need a doctor, but the sick. 32 I have not come to call the righteous, but sinners to repentance."

Luke 5:31-32

THE BLESSING AND OBEDIENCE

Welcome to Day 28

One aspect that I have enjoyed when it comes to these days of elevating is how the Holy Spirit will lead you to a bible book that you had no intention on exploring. Let us look at Deuteronomy 28:1 specifically the section on blessings. *28:1 And it shall come to pass, if thou shalt hearken diligently unto the voice of the LORD thy God, to observe and to do all his commandments which I command thee this day, that the LORD thy God will set thee on high above all nations of the earth ² And all these blessings shall come on thee, and overtake thee, if thou shalt hearken unto the voice of the LORD thy God.³ Blessed shalt thou be in the city, and blessed shalt thou be in the field.*

⁴ Blessed shall be the fruit of thy body, and the fruit of thy ground, and the fruit of thy cattle, the increase of thy kine, and the flocks of thy sheep. ⁵ Blessed shall be thy basket and thy store. ⁶ Blessed shalt thou be when thou comest in, and blessed shalt thou be when thou goest out. ⁷ The LORD shall cause thine enemies that rise up against thee to be smitten before thy face: they shall come out against thee one way and flee before thee seven ways.

8 The LORD shall command the blessing upon thee in thy storehouses, and in all that thou settest thine hand unto; and he shall bless thee in the land which the LORD thy God giveth thee.

9 The LORD shall establish thee a holy people unto himself, as he hath sworn unto thee, if thou shalt keep the commandments of the LORD thy God and walk in his ways. 10 And all people of the earth shall see that thou art called by the name of the LORD; and they shall be afraid of thee. 11 And the LORD shall make thee plenteous in goods, in the fruit of thy body, and in the fruit of thy cattle, and in the fruit of thy ground, in the land which the LORD sware unto thy fathers to give thee.

12 The LORD shall open unto thee his good treasure, the heaven to give the rain unto thy land in his season, and to bless all the work of thine hand: and thou shalt lend unto many nations, and thou shalt not borrow. 13 And the LORD shall make thee the head, and not the tail; and thou shalt be above only, and thou shalt not be beneath; if that thou hearken unto the commandments of the LORD thy God, which I command thee this day, to observe and to do them:

14 And thou shalt not go aside from any of the words which I command thee this day, to the right hand, or to the left, to go after other gods to serve them.15 But it shall come to pass, if thou wilt not hearken unto the voice of the LORD thy God, to observe to do all his commandments and his statutes which I command thee this day; that all these curses shall come upon thee, and overtake thee:

16 Cursed shalt thou be in the city, and cursed shalt thou be in the field. 17 Cursed shall be thy basket and thy store.18 Cursed shall be the fruit of thy body, and the fruit of thy land, the increase of thy kine, and the flocks of thy sheep.[19] *Cursed shalt thou be when thou comest in, and cursed shalt thou be when thou goest out.*

It is critical to remember that, while we can use the benefits in God's word to transform our lives, going against God's will, can also result in curses. The accuser, Satan, might use the sin as an entry point for curses into our life. Take confidence, as the Lord often advised Joshua, and meditate on his word day and night. Blessings are wonderful while they flow, but the true test is how you cope when everything around you seems to be collapsing. It is at these moments that you must confront hardship with the fruit of the word buried in your heart.

Remember that when we are blessed, we are held accountable for the capacity of stewardship bestowed upon us. When it comes to stewardship, there are so many biblical greats to consider. Joseph, who had a relationship with God and was able to interpret the Pharaoh's dream, saved Egypt and his family during the famine. David and the Ark of the Covenant. Joshua was enraged when someone from his camp stole spoils despite the Lord's warning. Eli serves as both father and priest to his sons finds it difficult to correct them and as a result loses his life.

Remember that the word of God, repentance, Jesus' blood, fasting, prayer, and the power of the Holy Spirit enable us to break demonic patterns and cycles. bringing them under our feet where they belong.

Elevation – Transformation = Stagnation

Thoughts Of Virtue

THINK OF AREAS IN YOUR LIFE THAT YOU CAN OBEY THE
WORD OF GOD MORE.

_____

_____

_____

_____

_____

_____

_____

_____

_____

_____

_____

_____

_____

*Be sober, be vigilant; because your adversary the devil, as a roaring
lion, walketh about, seeking whom he may devour*

1 Peter 5:8

SPIRITUAL DECAY

Welcome to Day 29

Today, I want to talk about an issue that may hit near to home for some of us–spiritual degeneration. Everybody has gone through times in their lives when they felt as though they were physically, emotionally, and even spiritually collapsing. It's a frightening and perplexing sensation that we might not be able to pinpoint the origin of. I declare and decree that you shall receive the anointing of the curse breaker today. Give those words time to sink in. Here for you is the curse breaker, the one who has the power to break you free from the bands of wickedness. The Lord is here to raise you up, regardless of what has led to your state of decline—whether it is psychologically, emotionally, physically, or spiritually.

We might not even be aware of the reason for our current situation, but nevertheless here we are. I want to encourage you today that you don't have to deal with it on your own. Think about the meaning of decay. (1). The dictionary states that, in general, decay refers to the process of becoming gradually damaged, worse, or less. (2). In a broader sense, decay can also refer to a decline in health, strength, or vigor.

Oh, my goodness this goes back to *1 John 3:2 Beloved, I pray that in every way you may succeed and prosper and be in good health [physically], just as [I know] your soul prospers [spiritually].*

Imagine if we spoke to one another like this daily. Literally if this was our proclamation over our loved ones and friends. The elder of the church is saying that spiritually you are full, and I pray that your soul can maintain your spiritual health or fullness. In my opinion, when we are spiritually depleted it shows in our physical health. When the soul is deeply wounded it can internally affect the cells in our body causing physical decay. May the very fullness of God's word spring up in you today like a well spring of life.

Look at Proverbs 16:22. *"Understanding is a wellspring of life unto him that hath it: but the instruction of fools is folly.*

I want you to proclaim this over yourself every day when you get out the bed, while you're getting dressed, or facing a difficult task remember to command your soul to prosper. **PROSPER SOUL PROSPER!** Let us break free from spiritual decay and allow God's blessings to guide us towards a brighter future. The word of God says, "My grace is sufficient for you, for my power is made perfect in weakness" (2 Corinthians 12:9). Let us lean on God's grace and let His power perfect us in our moments of weakness. Remember, you are not alone. God is with you, and He will never leave you nor forsake you. Now get up from this state of dilapidation and walk confidently into your future, with the grace and anointing of the curse breaker leading the way.

Thoughts Of Virtue

PROSPER SOUL PROSPER

_____
_____
_____
_____
_____
_____
_____
_____
_____
_____
_____
_____
_____
_____

My grace is sufficient for you, for my power is made perfect in weakness"

2 Corinthians 12:9

JESUS IS YOUR ADVOCATE

WELCOME TO DAY 30

During a global pandemic, many of us found ourselves struggling with feelings of loneliness and isolation. The physical distancing measures put in place to prevent the spread of Covid-19 left us separated from our loved ones and the comforting routines of our daily lives. While it may have felt like we were facing those challenges alone, there was one constant presence that remained by our side–Jesus, our Advocate.

In 1st John chapter 2, we are reminded that we have an Advocate in Jesus Christ, who intercedes for us with the Father. This may seem like a distant and abstract concept, but in times of loneliness and despair, it can be a source of great comfort and hope.

During that time, it was easy to feel forgotten and insignificant. We missed the interactions with our friends and family, the simple pleasures of going out to eat or attending church services. Even when we feel alone, we are never truly alone, for Christ is always with us. He sees our struggles and feels our pain. As our Advocate, Jesus stands beside us, ready to defend and support us when we feel weak.

Just as a lawyer advocate for their client in a court of law, Jesus advocates for us in the presence of God. He stands before the Father and reminds Him of His great sacrifice on the cross, and how His blood covers all our sins. Jesus is our defender, our refuge, and our Redeemer.

Thoughts Of Virtue

YOU ARE NOT DOING IT BY YOURSELF! YOU HAVE AN
ADVOCATE IN CHRIST

_____

_____

_____

_____

_____

_____

_____

_____

_____

_____

_____

_____

_____

I will love thee, O LORD, my strength. ² The LORD is my rock, and my fortress, and my deliverer; my God, my strength, in whom I will trust; my buckler, and the horn of my salvation, and my high tower.

Psalms 18:1

YOU ARE NOT ALONE

Welcome to day 31!

Can I tell you we are more than halfway there? Today, I want to talk to you more about Jesus being your advocate. Life can throw us some unexpected curveballs. Certainly, as I spoke on the previous day concerning the pandemic, it was indeed a curveball to all of us. From small daily challenges to major life-altering events, we all face situations where we need someone to stand by us, to fight for us, and to support us, and during these past couple of years it has been tough for so many of us.

Let us be real, not everyone is comfortable with being alone. Some people feel anxious or lost when they are left to deal with their own thoughts and emotions. In times of crisis, this need for human connection and support can become overwhelming. We have seen people turn to unhealthy coping mechanisms like drinking and overeating, but that is not the answer. It has been a tough time for all of us, and we have all needed some sort of outlet to deal with our emotions and fears.

What about those who have had to face the most challenging and traumatic situations during this time? The ones who have lost loved ones or have been separated from them, the ones who have had to grieve alone, and the ones who could not even say goodbye. We do not often talk about the impact that such experiences have on a person's mental and emotional well-being, but it is something that needs to be addressed.

In moments like these, we need to remember that we have an advocate in Jesus Christ. He is the hope of glory, the one who stands by us, and fights for us, even when we feel like we are alone. He knows our struggles, and He understands our pain. Christ is always there, listening to our prayers and advocating for our well-being. You may feel like no one cares about your struggles, or that you have been left to deal with them on your own. I want to remind you today that you have an advocate who knows you better than anyone else and has given His life for you. The Love of Yeshua knows no bounds and is here to carry your burdens and give you strength to face each day.

If you are going through a tough time, feel overwhelmed and alone, take comfort in knowing that Jesus is on your side. He will never leave you or forsake you. Let His love and grace be your comfort and strength and know that you are never alone. *You know that you are loved, valued, and never alone.*

Thoughts Of Virtue

ARE THERE MOMENTS WHEN YOU FELT LONELINESS CREEPING
IN? WHAT WAS YOUR RESPONSE?

_____

_____

_____

_____

_____

_____

_____

_____

_____

_____

_____

_____

_____

_____

Greater love hath no man than this, that a man lay down his life for his friends.

John 15:13

I'M NOT LOSING ANOTHER THING

Welcome TO Day 32

It is time to reflect on your past losses and find the determination to never fall into a comfortable state of losing again.

You cannot afford to become complacent about losing. There is enough in you for you to achieve your measure of greatness, now decide that enough is enough. It is time to say, "I'm not losing again." Whether you are part of a team or an individual in a constant state of defeat, it is time to shift your mindset from being a sore loser to a determined individual.

A sore loser is someone who handles defeat poorly and may even resort to cheating or causing harm to others in an attempt to win. There is a difference between having a losing streak and being a sore loser. When you experience loss after loss, it is easy to become discouraged and feel like giving up. Instead of sulking or becoming bitter, take a step back and analyze your past losses. Each loss is an opportunity to learn and grow.

It is easy to fall into a state of discouragement when you see others succeeding while you are still standing at the gate of defeat. Remember, everybody gets their turn. Your struggles have prepared you for your breakthrough. As challenging as it may be, do not let defeat and discouragement make you dead to your potential. Instead, let the dew of the morning, the refreshing river and breath of the Holy Spirit, revive and rejuvenate you.

You have the power to get up again. Like the man at the gate called Beautiful, do not be afraid to ask to be taken to the water. Let the healing power of God wash over you and propel you towards your destiny.

Today, as we reflect on Acts 3:6-13, remember to never become comfortable losing. Place a demand on your situation, and trust in the healing power of the blood of Jesus. And before you know it, you will step out of your losing season and into a season of victory and elevation.

Thoughts Of Virtue

WHAT AREAS IN YOUR LIFE MAKE YOU FEEL PARALIZED?

_____

_____

_____

_____

_____

_____

_____

_____

_____

_____

_____

_____

_____

_____

_____

_____

Then Peter said, Silver and gold have I none; but such as I have give I thee: In the name of Jesus Christ of Nazareth rise up and walk.

Acts 3:6

A KEEPER OF HIS WORD

Welcome to Day 33

Today's topic is centered around a powerful message that speaks to the core of our faith. It is a message that reminds us of the importance of keeping God's word, even in our darkest moments. It is a message that holds the key to perfecting our love for God. In Hebrew, the number 33 symbolizes promise, specifically the promise of eternal life. And on this 33rd day of elevation, we are reminded of God's promise to us and the importance of keeping our promises to Him.

The Book of 1 John 2:5-11 says, "But whoever keeps his word, in him truly the love of God is perfected. By this we may know that we are in him: whoever says he abides in him ought to walk in the same way in which he walked." This powerful verse speaks to the transformative power of keeping God's word. It is through our obedience to His word that we are truly able to experience the perfected love of God.

As we continue our journey of elevation, we may find ourselves in moments of weakness and doubt. We may feel overwhelmed by the enemy's attacks on our minds and emotions. But it is in those moments that we must choose to stand on the promises of God. It is in those moments that we must declare His word and continue to speak it, even when we do not feel like it. For when we make a conscious decision to keep God's word, He begins to perfect us in all areas of our lives. It is like filling up our spiritual gas tank with heavenly gasoline. The more we fill up, the more we can walk in the light and overcome darkness.

1 John 2: 7-8 says, "Beloved, I am writing you no new commandment, but an old commandment that you had from the beginning. The old commandment is the word that you have heard. At the same time, it is a new commandment that I am writing to you, which is true in him and in you, because the darkness is passing away and the true light is already shining. "What is this new commandment? Simply put, it is to abide in Christ and walk in His ways. As believers, we often look to our pastors and church leaders as role models, but this verse reminds us that Jesus is the ultimate model. I tell you, it is through abiding in Him that we can overcome darkness and walk in the light. Verse 11 of this passage also reminds us of the importance of loving our brothers and sisters in Christ. We must forgive and love others as we come into the light. It is an ongoing process, but through our love for others, we can walk with a clear conscience and not give the enemy any room to cause us to stumble.

On this 33rd day of elevation, don't you forget the power of speaking God's word. In closing, if we can make a conscious decision to keep His word The Father can grow us in areas of obedience and love for others, as we walk in the light and fulfill the promise of eternal life.

Thoughts Of Virtue

THINK OF ONE SCRIPTURE THAT BRINGS JOY& PEACE.

_____

_____

_____

_____

_____

_____

_____

_____

_____

_____

_____

_____

_____

_____

The light shines in the darkness, and the darkness has not overcome it.

John 1:5

FUNCTION VS FELLOWSHIP

We are now on day 34 of 50 Days of Elevation, and today we are talking about function versus fellowship.

I know it may sound confusing initially, but bear with me. On cue, you can function. You can fall right into line and do what is expected of you. Let me tell you, functioning is not your problem. It is the better part. Yes, learning how to sit still and wait patiently is where the real challenge lies.

Take the story of Lazarus, for example. When Jesus did not show up immediately to heal him, people got mad. They were impatient because Lazarus had already started to stink (yikes!). They could not understand the power that Jesus had to resurrect him. They were too used to seeing Jesus perform miracles and healing people without truly understanding the anointing that was upon his life. They were too familiar with him and did not respect the mantle that he carried. And let us be real, sometimes we are guilty of the same thing. We miss the better part because we are so caught up in looking for a function instead of focusing on fellowship. Instead of connecting with God and seeking His presence, we are too busy expecting Him to function according to our wants and needs. Just like Mary and Martha, who were so familiar with Jesus that they could not fully grasp the magnitude of his power. They were expecting him to function in a certain way, and when he did not, they were disappointed. They missed the miracle of Lazarus being brought back to life because they were too caught up in their own expectations.

Let us not forget about the other people who were waiting for Jesus to show up. They were too familiar with Him, expecting Him to function in a certain way. They were not listening for the shift, not waiting for the miracle of Lazarus going from stinking to living. They were too fixated on their own idea of how Jesus should function instead of being open to His miraculous power.

Take a moment to reflect, are we too familiar with God? Are we too caught up in looking for a specific function in our men and women of God, instead of understanding the true power and anointing they carry? Are we missing miracles because we do not expect the shift, the unexpected ways in which God can work? Let us learn to catch the prophetic, to listen for the sound and be open to the shifts that God brings. Let us not limit Him by expecting Him to function in ways that we want. Instead, let us be in fellowship with Him, seeking His presence and being open to His miraculous power at work. Just like death was not greater than Jesus, our problems and expectations should not limit God's power. Let us be in fellowship with Him, always open to His miraculous shifts in our lives.

Thoughts Of Virtue

IN WHAT WAYS HAVE YOU PUT GOD IN A BOX? GET HIM OUT
NOW!

_____

_____

_____

_____

_____

_____

_____

_____

_____

_____

_____

_____

_____

_____

*When Jesus heard that, he said, this sickness is not unto death, but
for the glory of God, that the Son of God might be glorified thereby*
John11:4

BEYOND THE BOX

Welcome to Day 35

Can you believe we are already on the 35th day? Time sure flies when you are on a journey of self-discovery and growth. I want to remind you not to miss the better part because you are too focused on the function. Are you ready? Let us tackle it together.

Now I want you to recall a time when you questioned someone's behavior or comments. Perhaps it was a friend, family member, or even a stranger. You couldn't help but wonder why they did that. What's the reasoning behind this?" It's only natural that we seek to comprehend and make sense of things. Sometimes, in our search for answers, we lose sight of the overall picture - the better part.

Think about it, when we are so fixated on trying to figure out the "why," we often miss the message being conveyed. Our minds are spinning, trying to process and comprehend the situation, and in the process, we miss out on the shift happening right before our eyes. We miss the opportunity to grow and evolve.

Why do we do this? Why do we get so caught up in trying to understand everything? Well, it could be because as people, we like to have control over our lives. We want to know why things happen, and we feel like if we understand, we can have a sense of control. Welp here is the thing, my friends, we are not meant to control everything. Sometimes, in our pursuit of understanding, we end up putting Jesus in a box.

Yes, you read that right - we put Jesus in a box. We try to understand His intentions and actions, and in doing so, we limit Him. We limit His power and ability to work in our lives. We try to fit Him into our human mindset, and in doing so, we miss the better part of what He has in store for us.

So, what is the solution? How can we avoid getting stuck in this cycle of trying to understand everything? Well, the answer is simple yet challenging - get Jesus out of the box. Allow Yeshua to work in your life in ways that you may not understand. Trust in His plan, even when it does not make sense to you. Here is the thing: God's ways are higher than our ways. He sees the bigger picture, and sometimes we just need to have faith and trust in His perfect timing and plans.

Thoughts Of Virtue

HOW HARD HAS IT BEEN TO TRUST?

_____

_____

_____

_____

_____

_____

_____

_____

_____

_____

_____

_____

_____

_____

_____

My son, attend to my words; incline thine ear unto my sayings.
Prov 4:20

THE POSITION AND THE MISSION

Welcome to Day 36

As we journey through our elevation, we must learn to listen and speak what the Holy Spirit desires for us to know, the position and the mission. It is not about constantly questioning and analyzing; it is about being attuned to the voice of God, accepting the download that He has for us. To do this, we must be still in His presence. We must learn to wait patiently, with focused eyes, attentive ears, and a postured heart. It is in these quiet moments that the voice of the Lord will soothe us and guide us towards our elevation.

In Luke 10:39, we see the contrast between Mary and Martha's positions. While Martha was busy with her duties, Mary sat at the feet of Jesus, mesmerized by His presence. Martha got upset, feeling like she was left to do all the work. But if we look closely, Mary had recognized the presence of the Holy One and got still in His presence, waiting for instruction. Do we recognize when the presence of the Lord enters the room? Are we too caught up in our functions and responsibilities that we miss His presence? Mary's posture of stillness and attentiveness to the Lord taught us an important lesson. She was not focused on how she needed to function, but rather on what her posture needed to be in His presence.

Let us reflect on this for a moment. When we sense the presence of God, sometimes we may feel the urge to shout or completely yield, and either is okay. What matters is recognizing His presence and being attuned to His message for us. We must not be caught up in trying to function like everyone else, but rather focus on our posture in His presence.

It is important to note that it is not wrong to have duties and responsibilities; however, we must remember to take a moment and bask in the presence of The Lord, allowing Him to guide and lead all our functions. When you find yourself in a similar situation as Martha, remember to choose the better part - recognizing and embracing the presence of God. Let us not get too caught up in the function that we miss the opportunity to be in the presence of the Holy One. As we continue our 50 Days of Elevation, let us keep our eyes, ears, and hearts focused and postured in His presence. My prayer is that catch a glimpse of the greatness God has in store for you. Stay elevated, children of the most- high God! Until next time, remember to always choose the best part.

Thoughts Of Virtue

IF DECLUTTERING YOUR MIND WAS A THING, WHAT WOULD
YOU GET RID OF?

_____

_____

_____

_____

_____

_____

_____

_____

_____

_____

_____

_____

_____

For who is greater, he who sits at the table, or he who serves? Is it not he who sits at the table? Yet I am among you as the One who serves.

Luke 22:27

TO FAMILIAR TO FELLOWSHIP

Welcome to Day 37

Today, let us dive into a topic that might catch some of us off guard: familial spirits and their functions in the life of a believer. Now, before we go any further, let us understand what familial spirits are. These are the spirits that run within our family bloodline, passed down from generations to generations. They can manifest in different ways, such as addiction, mental illness, or financial struggles.

Have you ever found yourself going to church, doing all the right churchy things, but not really understanding or receiving the message? That is because we are too busy functioning instead of fellowshipping. Fellowshipping allows us to connect deeper with God and receive what He has in store for us. When we only focus on functioning, we miss the deeper meaning and purpose behind it all. Think about it, how many times have you been in church and not really paid attention to the message because you were too busy performing your duties? It happens all too often, and we do not even realize it.

Over the next few weeks, let us make a conscious effort to move away from the familiarity of how we function in our ministerial roles and our church attendance. Let us truly seek the ministry of fellowship. This is when we can truly receive from our pastors and leaders because our pursuit is being connected to the spirit of the covenant keeping God only and not just going through the motions. We can see the parallels in our everyday lives in ministry. We may not die to ourselves because we have learned how to function in our gifts. We think we are living in the power of the Holy Spirit, but really, we are just functioning in our gifts. Let us take speaking in tongues, for example. It is a beautiful gift from the Holy Spirit, but if we are not yielded to Christ Jesus the anointed one and living a holy life, it is just another function that we have learned. It is not a true manifestation of the Holy Spirit within us. What about pastors and leaders who struggle with addictions or other sins? They may have a way with words and can preach the house down, but are they truly yielded to God? Can they live out what they preach, or do they find ways to justify their actions?

This is where familiar spirits come into play. These spirits have learned how to blend in and deceive us. I once had a woman tell me that she had been a cocaine addict for 30 years, all while serving in ministry. Can you imagine the torment and mental struggle she must have been going through? Yet, she continued to function in her role without anyone in the church operating in the spirit of discernment to see her pain. It is time for us to get away from just how we function and look beyond the surface of people. We need to ask God to open our eyes and let us see the truth. Let the eyes of our understanding come forth in Jesus' name.

In closing, as we continue this journey towards elevation, let us remember to not only function, but also fellowship with God. Let us ask the Holy Spirit to reveal any familiar spirits in our families and ourselves so that we can break free and live in the fullness of God's love and grace.

Thoughts Of Virtue

WHAT DID I MISS BECAUSE I WAS TOO FAMILIAR?

_____

_____

_____

_____

_____

_____

_____

_____

_____

_____

_____

_____

_____

_____

But you are those who have continued with Me in My trials. [29] And I bestow upon you a kingdom, just as My Father bestowed one upon Me.

Luke 22:28

TRAPPINGS

Welcome to day 38!

We have come a long way, and we are closer to our destination, but some of us might be wondering, why can't we reach the next dimension in Christ? I know there is a next level, a higher place that we are supposed to be in, but every time we get close, something seems to hold us back. It is almost as if there is something hindering my way.

In Galatians 5:1-8, Paul asked a crucial question, "Who hindered you?" It is a question that we must ask ourselves as we move through the remaining days. Who or what is hindering us from moving forward? Who is interfering and preventing us from obeying the truth? As I was seeking guidance from the Holy Spirit, He spoke these words to me. "Look for the trappings." What are the trappings that are holding us back from moving to the next dimension? The trappings that come with a hindering spirit are deception and false teachings. You see, when we first got saved and filled with the Holy Spirit, we were on fire for God. We were running the race well, but then something happened. We began to reason amongst ourselves, and that is when the deception starts to seep in. We deceive ourselves with our own thoughts, and that is when the hindering spirits gain power over us.

Verse 8 says, "This deceptive persuasion is not from Him who called you to freedom in Christ." Friends, we must be careful not to let false teachings and deceptive thoughts mislead us and pervert the true message of faith. We cannot simply use God's grace as an excuse to continue living in sin.

It is time to break free from these hindering spirits and their trappings. We need deliverance and a renewal of our minds. Remember, a little leaven can leaven the whole batch. One false teaching, one deceptive thought can lead us astray and derail our spiritual journey. You cannot allow the enemy to hold you back any longer. Seek deliverance from any hindering spirits in your life and ask the Holy Spirit to renew your mind and guide you on your journey. Let us not be deceived by false teachings, but instead, let us obey the truth and continue running towards the next dimension in Christ.

Do not let a hindering spirit stop you from reaching your full potential in God. He has called us to a place of freedom and victory, and we must not allow anything to hold us back. Keep moving forward, and trust in the Lord to guide you to your next dimension in Christ.

Thoughts Of Virtue

WHO OR WHAT HAS HINDERED YOU?

_____

_____

_____

_____

_____

_____

_____

_____

_____

_____

_____

_____

_____

_____

_____

One man esteemed one day above another: another esteemed every day alike. Let every man be fully persuaded in his own mind

Romans 14:5

A LITTLE LEAVEN

Welcome to Day 39

You are almost at the finish line. I would like to pick up from a different view of hindrances that you may have encountered at some point in life. Let us begin.

Are you tired of feeling stuck and hindered in your life? Frustrated by the constant distractions and obstacles that seem to hold you back from reaching your true potential? Well, my friend, it is time to take a stand and move beyond everything that tries to hold you back.

In his letter to the Galatians, the apostle Paul addresses a crucial issue that is still relevant today—the deceptive persuasion of false teachers. These teachers were causing chaos and confusion among the believers, trying to turn them against their leader and perverting the concept of faith. Paul warns the Galatians, just as he warns us, that a little leaven, or false teaching, can have a harmful impact on our lives. It only takes a slight inclination to error to hinder our progress and mislead us from the truth. Have you ever found yourself in a situation where someone is constantly pointing out the flaws of your leader, trying to sway you to their side? That is the spirit of Kora and Miriam at work, and it is a dangerous trap that can keep us trapped in mediocrity. Paul encourages the Galatians, and us, to have confidence in the Lord and not adopt any views that are contrary to the truth. He reminds us that there will be a penalty for those who try to hinder our progress and keep us from moving forward in our faith.

How can we overcome these hindrances and move beyond where we are? It starts with having confidence in Christ and seeking His guidance and direction. It also involves actively walking in the power of the Holy Spirit and responding to His leading. When we do, we can resist the desire of our sinful nature and experience true freedom and progress as believers.

Paul also reminds us of the danger of using our freedom as an opportunity for selfishness and worldliness. Instead, he encourages us to love and serve one another, fulfilling the law of loving our neighbor as ourselves. When we allow love to guide our actions, we will not only benefit ourselves but also those around us.

As we seek to move beyond everything that tries to hinder our lives, it's essential to remember that progress does not come easy. We may face persecution and obstacles along the way, but it is through fasting and prayer that we tap into the power of God and see miracles happen in our lives.

Ultimately, it is up to us to take a stand, have confidence in Christ, and walk in the power and guidance of the Holy Spirit. I encourage you to not let anything or anyone hold you back from reaching your full potential and experiencing the life of abundance that Jesus the savior has for you.

Thoughts Of Virtue

WHAT THE LEAVEN?

_____

_____

_____

_____

_____

_____

_____

_____

_____

_____

_____

_____

_____

Finally, brethren, whatsoever things are true, whatsoever things are honest, whatsoever things are just, whatsoever things are pure, whatsoever things are lovely , whatsoever things are of good report; if there be any virtue, and if there be praise, think on these things.

Phil 4:8

CODE UPGRADE FROM HEAVEN

Welcome to Day 40

Have you ever been in a situation where you were comfortable with your living conditions but deep down you knew that there was something more for you? That is exactly how I felt on day 40 of my 50 days of elevation journey. Little did I know, I was about to receive a code upgrade from heaven that would open doors of elevation for me.

As believers, we often get too comfortable in our current state and forget that God has bigger plans for us. We must be willing to let go of things that are not aligned with His will to receive spiritual upgrades in our lives. Some may wonder, why do we need upgrades? The answer is simple—just like how a house needs to be constantly upgraded to meet safety standards and regulations, our souls also need to be upgraded to align with God's plans for us. As I was going through this process of a spiritual upgrade, I could not help but think of Psalm 127.

This psalm talks about how unless the Lord is in charge, our efforts will go in vain. It compares the walls of a city to the walls of our souls and reminds us that without God's protection, even the strongest walls are useless. Just like how a house built in the eighties may not meet the code standards of today, our old ways may not align with what God has in store for us now. That is when we need an upgrade in our souls to elevate us to where God wants us to be.

Here is the good news — the way insurance companies provide coverage for code upgrades in our homes when we have a specific endorsement, Christ is our insurance carrier. He is the GC (General Contractor) of our lives, and it is His duty to ensure that we are up to code with His plans.

Why do we doubt our coverage? Why do we limit ourselves when we have the Almighty God on our side? We need to remember that as the children of God, we are as The Lord's property, and He will do everything in His power to bring us up to code. As we allow God to upgrade us, we must also remember that the process may involve tearing down. This may be uncomfortable, but it is necessary for our spiritual growth and elevation. When we trust in God's process, we can confidently declare, "My upgrade is upon me!" In this hour, let us not be like those who oppose the inspector's recommendation and refuse to make necessary changes. Let us yield to the Father and follow His plans, because only then can we truly be elevated to new heights. As you continue your 50-day elevation journey, let us be grateful for the code upgrade that God has given us access to. I encourage you, as a believer, to seek God's upgrades in your life, for it is the key to your elevation. Remember, the walls of your soul must be up to code for you to reach new levels. Psalm 127 says it perfectly — *"Unless the Lord builds the house, the builders labor in vain." It is essential to trust the Lord's plan and allow Him to upgrade you for His glory. Are you ready to be elevated?*

Thoughts Of Virtue

ARE YOU READY FOR YOUR UPGRADE?

_____

_____

_____

_____

_____

_____

_____

_____

_____

_____

_____

_____

_____

Teacher, which is the greatest commandment in the Law?" [37] _And Jesus replied to him, "'YOU SHALL LOVE THE LORD YOUR GOD WITH ALL YOUR HEART, AND WITH ALL YOUR SOUL, AND WITH ALL YOUR MIND.'_ [38] _This is the first and greatest commandment._

Matt 22:36

MY BODY: HIS TEMPLE

Welcome back to our 50 days of elevation encounter.

Can you believe it is already day forty-one? We are almost at the end of this amazing journey of growth and elevation. Today, I want to talk about something that may sound a bit unconventional. We are going to discuss ourselves, our bodies, and how it is the temple of the Lord. Yes, you read that right. Our bodies, regardless of what your walls may look like or how strong of a force you may be, your body is the temple of the Lord. Here is why this is such an important realization - if The Lord Jesus–The chief cornerstone built it, He admires what he built. Think about it, when a contractor builds a house, they take pride in their work. They pay attention to every little detail, from the crown molding to the trusses to the type of brick used. And that is because they have invested their blood, sweat, and tears into creating something beautiful.

In the same way, our creator, God, has built us with care and admiration. He sees us as his prized possessions, his handiwork. Very much like a contractor takes pride in their creation, God too, takes pride in us. That is why it says in 1 Corinthians 6:19 *"Do you not know that your bodies are temples of the Holy Spirit, who is in you, whom you have received from God? You are not your own."* This verse is a reminder that we are not just flesh and bones, but we are also spiritual beings, with a divine purpose and a duty to take care of our bodies. Sadly, many of us neglect this responsibility. We do not give our bodies the proper rest, nourishment, and maintenance they need. We overwork ourselves, constantly fearing that we will fall short and not be able to provide for ourselves. But here is the thing, God wants his loved ones to get their proper rest.

Psalm 127 says, *"Unless the Lord watches over the city, the watchmen stand guard in vain. In vain you rise early and stay up late, toiling for food to eat - for he grants sleep to those he loves."* This verse reminds us that true success and abundance comes from the Lord, and if we trust in him, we can rest and find peace in his protection and providence.

As we run this race towards elevation, let us not forget that our bodies are temples of the Holy Spirit. Let us take care of ourselves, physically and spiritually, and give our bodies the rest it needs to sustain us. Think of a house that needs regular maintenance and sometimes, even an upgrade. We too should consider regular maintenance. We must let go of any negativity, hurt, and burdens weighing us down, and allow God to remodel us into the best versions of ourselves.

In thought, let us take pride in the temple of the Lord, and give it the care and attention it deserves. Start a daily walk, or regimen that caters to your physical as well as working and building your spiritual and watch all of heaven come to your aid to help you fulfill your divine purpose.

Thoughts Of Virtue

HOW CAN I BE A STEWARD OVER HIS TEMPLE?

_____

_____

_____

_____

_____

_____

_____

_____

_____

_____

_____

Therefore whosoever heareth these sayings of mine, and doeth them, I will liken him unto a wise man, which built his house upon a rock: 25 And the rain descended, and the floods came, and the winds blew, and beat upon that house; and it fell not: for it was founded upon a rock. 26 And everyone that heareth these sayings of mine, and doeth them not, shall be likened unto a foolish man, which built his house upon the sand: 27 And the rain descended, and the floods came, and the winds blew, and beat upon that house; and it fell: and great was the fall of it.

Matt 7:24-27

THE HOLY SPIRIT WILL ALWAYS KNOCK

We are on day 42 of 50 days of elevation.

Congratulations on making it this far! I want to share with you some powerful words that the Lord spoke to me.

I woke up on September 26, 2022, to the sound of knocks. At first, I did not immediately get up, but the knocks grew louder, and I knew I had to pay attention. The Lord revealed to me that the Holy Spirit will always ask for permission to come into our lives, unlike the thief who will forcefully find a way in.

It got me thinking, how many times have we opened the door for the enemy without even realizing it? We may think we are in control, but the enemy has snuck in and is causing havoc without our knowledge. But fear not, my friend, for we have been given the power to resist the devil and kick him out.

The Lord also reminds me of something powerful that Pastor Anthony and I prayed over - Matthew 7:7-12, where Jesus tells us *"Ask and it will be given to you; seek and you will find knock and the door will be opened to you."* The Lord wants to elevate our lives, but we need to be careful to distinguish between His voice and the voice of the enemy. It is important to remember that the Holy Spirit and angels will always knock and ask for permission, while the enemy will kick down our doors and squat in our lives. We must not allow these squatters to take over what belongs to us. Instead, we must go to the authorities (God) and kick them out.

1 Peter 5:8 says, "Be alert and of sober mind. Your enemy the devil prowls around like a roaring lion looking for someone to devour." We must always be vigilant and on guard, ready to resist the enemy and stand firm in our faith.

Take the time today and reflect on just how far you have come. Let us always be mindful of the Holy Spirit's gentle knocks on our doors, and never allow the enemy to gain control over our lives. With the power of God, we can overcome any attack and be elevated to new levels.

Keep pushing forward, keep praying, and keep seeking the guidance of the Holy Spirit. I am excited to see what the final days of this journey will bring for you. I cannot wait to hear your personal testimony. May God continue to bless and elevate you in every aspect of your life.

Thoughts Of Virtue

WHO/WHAT FORECEFULLY ENTERED YOUR LIFE?

_____

_____

_____

_____

_____

_____

_____

_____

_____

_____

_____

_____

_____

"Be alert and of sober mind. Your enemy the devil prowls around like a roaring lion looking for someone to devour." We must always be vigilant and on guard, ready to resist the enemy and stand firm in our faith.

1 Peter 5:8

ARISE SHINE

Day 43 of the 50 Days of Elevation has been a powerful one.

If you are feeling down or struggling with depression. With only seven days left. We will be looking into Isaiah 60 and understanding the brilliance of God's glory that can call you forth from the depths of depression.

Depression is a heavy weight that can keep you in a downward position, making it hard to even come to the altar or commit to your faith. Look in Isaiah 60, the word of God tells us to arise and shine, for His light and glory have come upon us. It is important to note that it is the glory of the Lord that lifts us from depression. Yes, you heard that right. The Glory of The Lord revealed in the heart of a believer is the antidote to depression.

Imagine being in a dark room all day, every day. It can have a serious effect on your mood and outlook on life. I often remind my children to open their curtains in the morning and let the light in. The only time the curtains should be closed is when the sun goes down. In the same way, we should not dwell in spiritual darkness. It brings us down and affects our overall well-being. God wants us to arise from spiritual depression and step into a new life filled with radiance and brilliance. It is the kind of brilliance that comes with the glory of God. When I first started learning about the glory, I would pray for the brilliance of God's glory to come upon us. Let me tell you, the glory of God carries immense brilliance and value. It carries weight, which is often referred to as the Kabod.

The way a diamond shines and reflects its value through its brilliance, the same goes for us with the glory of God. There is no brilliance or no value without the glory and we will lack value in the Kingdom of God. We must open our hearts and minds to the brilliance of God's glory and watch as it overrides depression and brings us to a new level of elevation. Let us a rise and shine with the light of Jesus Christ.

Thoughts Of Virtue

WHEN WAS THE LAST TIME YOU CONSIDERED YOUR VALUE?

_____

_____

_____

_____

_____

_____

_____

_____

_____

_____

_____

_____

_____

Arise, shine, for your light has come, and the glory of the LORD rises upon you. See, darkness covers the earth and thick darkness is over the peoples, but the LORD rises upon you and his glory appears over you. Nations will come to your light, and kings to the brightness of your dawn.

Isaiah 60

THE GLORILESS CHURCH

Grace and peace be unto you this day! Congratulations on reaching Day 44 of the 50 Days of elevation. We have come a long way, and I am so proud of you for staying committed to this journey of spiritual growth.

Today, I want to talk to you about something that may be a tough pill to swallow, but it is a message that needs to be heard. It is about choosing the right church and not settling for one that is dead. *As Ephesians 6:12 says, "For we do not wrestle against flesh and blood, but against principalities, against powers, against the rulers of the darkness of this age, against spiritual hosts of wickedness in the heavenly places."*

It is a sad reality that there are churches out there where the power of Jesus Christ is not being revealed. Many people settle and go to these churches where there is no glory, no presence of God. When you go to a church with no glory, you will not see the currency of the Kingdom of Heaven in that place. You will not experience the brilliance of God's glory. And that is why it is important to be in the right place. Who wants to go to church or attend a service and leave with the same weight they came in with? No one, I am sure. Unfortunately, this is the case for many people who go to churches with no glory. They leave spiritually depressed and unchanged.

When we are in the presence of the Lord Jesus, His glory causes us to arise from the low place we were in. Isaiah 60 verse two says, "For behold, the darkness shall cover the earth, and deep darkness the people; but the Lord will arise over you, and His glory will be seen upon you." Today, I ask you, what do you look like these days? Do you look like someone who walks with a man or woman of God? Are you producing fruits that resemble the ministries and teachings you are under? As Joshua 1:3 says, "Every place that the sole of your foot will tread upon I have given you, as I said to Moses." My dear friends, it does not matter what darkness tries to cover the earth. It does not matter about the state of the world, the rise and fall of gas prices, or the spiritual wickedness in high places. We should not be affected by these things, for we are children of God and His glory is upon us.

Do not be surprised when you see people around you in a state of spiritual darkness. Just as the scripture says above in Isaiah 60:2 *"But the Lord will rise upon you. and His glory will be seen upon you."* We are called to stand out and shine beyond darkness.

I want to share a personal testimony with you. At the start of the pandemic, our church was led to go to Hilton Head, SC. We worshipped and prayed on the beach during the height of the pandemic, and not even one of us came back with COVID. In fact, the Lord blessed us in that place, and I would not be surprised if He sent us back there to set the captive free once again.

Please remember that we are called to be the light in this dark world. Let us not settle for worship experiences that are dead. Seek out places where the glory of God is revealed, and His power is evident, and we will all continue to walk in the fullness of God's glory and produce abundance that resembles the Kingdom of Heaven. Stay blessed!

Elevation – Transformation = Stagnation

Thoughts Of Virtue

DID YOU STAY TO LONG? WHAT WILL IT TAKE FOR YOU TO
LEAVE?

_____

_____

_____

_____

_____

_____

_____

_____

_____

_____

_____

_____

_____

*The Son radiates God's own glory and expresses the very character
of God, and he sustains everything by the mighty power of his
command. When he had cleansed us from our sins, he sat down in
the place of honor at the right hand of the majestic God in heaven.*

Heb 1:3

LUKEWARM AND STILL COLD

Today, during Day 45 of 50 Days of Elevation.

I came across an intriguing scripture from the book of Isaiah. It was Isaiah 60:6-10, and yes, we are still in Isaiah. Often, we rush through scripture, but I discern the importance of kind of hammering this point home. Flow with me while we milk this scripture a bit more.

The verse that caught my attention was, *"A multitude of camels shall cover you, the young camels of Midian and Ephah; all those from Sheba shall come. They shall bring gold and frankincense and shall proclaim the praise of the Lord." (Isaiah 60:6 ESV)* This verse talks about how wherever the glory of God is revealed, the wealth of the world flows towards it. It made me think about the importance of being in a church where the power of Jesus Christ is truly present.

In the modern world, we often see churches that focus more on building their own wealth and prosperity rather than glorifying God and spreading His love. They may have fancy buildings, huge tithes, and well-dressed pastors, but is the true power of Christ being revealed in those places? Are people experiencing miracles and transformations in their lives? If so then you are encountering the kingdom of God.

This verse from Isaiah reminds us that the true measure of a church's success is not in its material possessions, but in the presence of God's glory. When the glory of God is revealed in a place, people will be drawn towards it. Not just to see the outward appearance, but to experience the love, joy, and peace that comes with knowing Jesus.

As believers, we should not settle for a church where the power of God is not evident. We should seek out a place where the Holy Spirit is moving, where lives are being transformed, where people are being healed, and where the Word of God is being preached with authority. The true wealth is–in the presence of God. Now, I am not saying that church is the only place where we can experience God's glory. We can encounter Him in our homes, in nature, and in our quiet moments with Him. Being in a community of believers who are seeking and experiencing His glory together can be a truly uplifting and transformative experience. I digress, do not settle for a lukewarm church, a place where we just go through the motions and leave unchanged. Let us seek out the glory of God and be a part of a church where He is truly present. Because wherever the brilliance of His glory is, the wealth of the world or nations will surely follow.

Thoughts Of Virtue

WHAT KIND OF CHURCH COMMUNITY ARE YOU LOOKING FOR?

_____

_____

_____

_____

_____

_____

_____

_____

_____

_____

_____

_____

_____

For whoever desires to save his life will lose it, but whoever loses his life for My sake and the gospel's will save it. [36] For what will it profit a man if he gains the whole world, and loses his own soul?

Mark 8:35

I AM THE SOIL OF THE KINGDOM

Welcome to day forty-six!

Hey everyone! Today, let us explore a conversation from the Bible that talks about the refreshing and reviving power of Jesus through revival. We will be looking at John 3 and how Jesus and Nicodemus's conversation reveals the true ministry of Christ and the importance of being born again.

First off, let us look at Nicodemus. He was a Pharisee, a ruler of the Jews, who came to Jesus by night. And what did he say? *"We know that you are a teacher sent by God."* That right there is the first sign of someone carrying the ministry of Jesus Christ - there is evidence of the God they serve. Nicodemus and the other Jews saw Jesus' miracles and acknowledged that God must be with Him. There was a trail of evidence and testimonies left behind by Jesus, confirming His ministry.

Jesus' response to Nicodemus is what really caught my attention. He says, *"Truly, truly, I say to you, unless one is born again, he cannot see the kingdom of God."* In other words, you may have all the evidence and recognition, but if you have not been spiritually transformed and renewed, you cannot truly understand or enter the kingdom of God.

You see, revival is all about being revived, brought back to life. Jesus, through His sacrifice and resurrection, offers us this revival. But it is not just a onetime thing. He wants to constantly refresh us, restore us, and renew our faith.

Going back to the conversation between Jesus and Nicodemus, it is interesting to see how everything Nicodemus said was accurate, yet Jesus' response focused on being born again. It is like when someone tells you how great you are at praying or prophesying, and you start to get gassed up. Jesus is saying, all of that is great, but unless you have been spiritually transformed and renewed, it is not enough.

Today, let us reflect on our own lives. Have we been truly born again, spiritually transformed, and renewed? Revival is not just about experiencing miracles in the church, but it is also about evidence of a transformed life. Let us continue to seek God and allow Him to revive and refresh us, so that we can be a living testimony of His power and love.

Thoughts Of Virtue

WITH ALL THAT I KNOW, AM I TEACHBLE?

_____

_____

_____

_____

_____

_____

_____

_____

_____

_____

_____

_____

_____

_____

_____

_____

_____

Jesus told her, I am the resurrection and the life.[a] Anyone who believes in me will live, even after dying.

John 11:25

WATER&SPIRIT

Welcome to Day 47

We are in the last stretch, let us continue our study through the Book of John. We come to chapter 3, a pivotal moment in the ministry of Jesus. In this chapter, we see a conversation between Jesus and Nicodemus, a prominent Pharisee, and a member of the Jewish ruling council. Nicodemus had likely heard about the miracles and teachings of Jesus and was curious to find out more.

Little did Nicodemus know that this encounter would leave him completely stunned and leave us with a powerful message about being born of water and spirit. As we dive into this conversation between Jesus and Nicodemus, we can imagine Nicodemus' jaw dropping when *Jesus tells him that to enter the kingdom of God, one must be born again.*

Nicodemus, a learned man with great knowledge and intelligence, was confused by Jesus' statement. He could not fathom how a person could enter their mother's womb to be born again. His smarts and intelligence suddenly seemed insignificant in front of Jesus' words. Jesus was not talking about a physical rebirth; He was referring to a spiritual rebirth.

In verse five, Jesus clarifies by saying, "I assure you, unless one is born of water and the Spirit, he cannot enter the kingdom of God." This left Nicodemus and possibly even us with more questions. What does it mean to be born of water and spirit? Is it enough to just physically be baptized with water?

To answer this, we look at the testimony of John the Baptist in *John 1:27*. John understood his assignment was to prepare the way for Jesus and to baptize with water. John also knew that there was someone coming after him, someone who would baptize with the Holy Spirit and fire. Jesus' statement to Nicodemus was a foreshadowing of the fulfillment of this prophecy. He was telling Nicodemus that it is not enough to just be physically baptized with water, one must also be spiritually baptized with the Holy Spirit to enter the kingdom of God. This principle still applies to us today. We must be born again, not just of water, but also of the Spirit. We cannot rely on our own intelligence or good deeds to gain entry into the kingdom of God. It is only through the saving grace of Jesus Christ and the indwelling of the Holy Spirit that we can be born again and have a place in the kingdom of God.

As we reflect on this conversation between Jesus and Nicodemus, let us ask ourselves, have we truly been born of water and spirit? Have we accepted Jesus as our Lord and Savior and allowed the Holy Spirit to transform our hearts and minds?

May the testimony of John the Baptist and the words of Jesus in *John 3:5* inspire us to seek a spiritual rebirth and deepen our relationship with God. Let us remember that being born of water and spirit is the only way to enter into the kingdom of God. If you have not already confessed Christ as your Lord and savior no better time than to do it than now!

Thoughts Of Virtue

WHAT DOES IT MEAN TO BE BORN OF WATER AND SPIRIT?

_____

_____

_____

_____

_____

_____

_____

_____

_____

_____

_____

_____

_____

_____

_____

*If you openly declare that Jesus is Lord and believe in your heart
that God raised him from the dead, you will be saved.*

Romans 10:9

PRAYER OF SALVATION

WELCOME TO DAY 48

Heavenly Father, I come to acknowledge you as Lord over my life. I believe in my heart that you died on the cross and rose from the grave. I welcome you into my life, to be made new. I will share with others about my salvation. Thank you, Jesus!

As a Christian, one of the most powerful and transformative moments in my life was when I prayed the prayer of salvation, also known as the prayer of confession or sinners' prayer. It was a pivotal moment that changed the trajectory of my life and ushered me into a deeper relationship with Christ. In this moment, I want to focus on one verse that is often included in the prayer of salvation - Romans 10:9.

Romans 10:9 says, "If you declare with your mouth, 'Jesus is Lord,' and believe in your heart that God raised him from the dead, you will be saved." This verse is the foundation of the prayer of salvation. It acknowledges Jesus as Lord over our lives and affirms our belief in his death, burial, and resurrection. What exactly does it mean to declare Jesus as Lord and believe in his resurrection?

To declare something means to proclaim it loudly and confidently. In this case, it is declaring Jesus as the Lord of our lives. This is more than just acknowledging his existence or saying a quick prayer, it is surrendering all control and authority to him. It is a conscious decision to make Jesus the leader of our lives and to follow his teachings. Believing in the resurrection of Jesus is also a crucial aspect of the prayer of salvation. The resurrection is an integral part to our faith as Christians. It shows that Jesus has power over death and that he is indeed the Son of God. When we believe in the resurrection, we are acknowledging Jesus as our savior and putting our trust in him to save us from our sins.

The prayer of salvation is not a magical formula that guarantees a perfect life, free from troubles and trials. It is a sincere prayer of repentance and a conscious decision to follow Jesus. It is an admission of our sins and a plea for forgiveness. It is an invitation for Jesus to come into our lives and make us new. I remember the day I prayed the prayer of salvation. I was overwhelmed by a sense of peace and love that I had never experienced before. My burdens were lifted, and a weight lifted off my chest. It was a moment of transformation and a new beginning. If you have not prayed the prayer of salvation, I encourage you to do so. It is a powerful and life-changing prayer that can transform your life. You can use the sample prayer provided at the beginning of this post or pray from your heart. Remember, there are no specific formulas or words that guarantee salvation. It is all about a genuine surrender of your life to Jesus.

Thoughts Of Virtue

HOW DO YOU FEEL NOW THAT YOU HAVE RECEIVED CHRIST INTO YOUR LIFE?

_____

_____

_____

_____

_____

_____

_____

_____

_____

_____

_____

_____

_____

_____

For it is by believing in your heart that you are made right with God, and it is by openly declaring your faith that you are saved. [11] As the Scriptures tell us, "Anyone who trusts in him will never be disgraced.

Romans 10:10-11

EVERY SEED PRODUCES AFTER ITS OWN KIND

Welcome to day 49 of 50 days of elevation!

As we near the end of this journey, the Lord has revealed something powerful and eye-opening about the supernatural manifestation of His presence. As I was in Nashville, I heard testimonies from the people about their encounters with the river of God. But what caught my attention was not the water, but the fire within it. The people shared how they fell out when they stepped into the river of God, not because of the water, but because of the fire. They described feeling a burning sensation as they approached the woman of God, and as she stirred the water and sent its current towards them, they fell under the fire.

Now one might ask, how can a river be on fire? Even someone with a Nicodemus mindset would find it hard to understand. The Lord opened my eyes to this truth - the river of God is not just water; it is a river of fire. Last year, the Lord gave me the river of God for revival, but it was only this year that I truly understood its power. When one encounters the river of God one encounters the fire of God within the river. This supernatural river of fire is a symbol of the holy spirit-led life we are called to live. Jesus explained this concept in John 3:5-6 when he said, "unless you are born of water and the spirit, you cannot enter the kingdom of God. That which is born of flesh is flesh, and that which is born of the spirit is spirit." In other words, our physical bodies are merely physical, but when we are born of the spirit, we produce spiritual fruits. Just like how every seed produces after its own kind, if we sow seeds of the spirit, we will produce a spiritual harvest. If we sow seeds of the flesh, we will reap a fleshly harvest. This is why Jesus tells Nicodemus to not be surprised when he sees the supernatural manifestation of the spirit, for it is a result of being born of water and the spirit. It is important to check what kind of "seeds" we are sowing in our lives. Are we sowing seeds of brokenness and weakness, or are we sowing seeds of confidence in Christ and being led by the Holy Spirit? Our actions and intentions matter, as they determine the type of harvest we will reap.

Continue this journey of elevation. Let us be mindful of our thoughts, actions, and intentions. Let us strive to sow seeds of the spirit, so we can reap a bountiful harvest and truly experience the fullness of God's presence in our lives. May we always be holy spirit-led and walk confidently in Christ. Amen.

Thoughts Of Virtue

WHAT FRUIT DO YOU DESIRE TO SEE AFTER THIS?

_____

_____

_____

_____

_____

_____

_____

_____

_____

_____

_____

_____

_____

_____

And God said, Let the earth bring forth grass, the herb yielding seed, and the fruit tree yielding fruit after his kind, whose seed is in itself, upon the earth: and it was so.

Genesis 1:11

TRANSFORMATION

YOU DID IT!

As you reach the last day of your elevation journey, it is time to reflect on your transformation and renewal that has taken place. It has been a long 50 days, but now you stand ready to embrace the new heights and new dimensions. Jesus says, "Do not be surprised that I have told you, you must be born again, reborn from above, spiritually sanctified." These words from John 1:7 hold deep meaning as you look back at your journey of elevation. You have not only been born again, but also spiritually transformed, renewed, and sanctified. These are the four seeds that should be evident in the life of every believer who professes to be born again.

To be reborn from above means to be transformed spiritually. This transformation is crucial, but it does not end there. It has to be maintained. Just like a vehicle needs regular maintenance to function, your spiritual transformation needs to be nurtured continuously. If you ignore the upkeep of your vehicle, it will eventually break down and require a complete overhaul. Similarly, if you neglect the maintenance of your spiritual transformation, you may experience stagnation or even backslide.

You may have heard the phrase "blow a head gasket" when referring to a car's engine failure. This situation often occurs when a car is not adequately maintained and needs a new engine. In the same way, when you neglect the upkeep of your spiritual transformation, you may "blow a head gasket" and require a complete reset through repentance. You see, spiritual transformation is not a one-time fix. It is an ongoing process that requires your attention and effort every day. You may have felt renewed and free after your first transformation, but that is just the start. You need to be renewed every day and strive to live a holy, set-apart life. Perhaps you did not fully understand the concept of sanctification before your elevation journey. To be sanctified means to be holy, set apart, and consecrated. It is a call to live a life dedicated to God, following His commandments and will. It is not an easy task, but it is essential for your spiritual growth and transformation.

As you stand at this pivotal moment in your life, take a moment to reflect on your transformation and renewal, and thank the Holy Spirit for guiding you. But also, remember to stay vigilant in maintaining your spiritual life to avoid any potential "blown head gaskets." Let your elevation journey be a reminder that spiritual transformation is a continuous process, and you must strive to be renewed daily and live a life of sanctification.

Thoughts Of Virtue

DO YOU FEEL TRANSFORMED?

_____

_____

_____

_____

_____

_____

_____

_____

_____

_____

_____

_____

Go therefore and make disciples of all nations, baptizing them in the name of the Father and of the Son and of the Holy Spirit, teaching them to observe all that I have commanded you. And behold, I am with you always, to the end of the age."

Matt 28:19

CONCLUSION

I am proud of you for making it this far, and I know that you will continue to soar. Congratulations on completing your elevation journey. May you continue to grow and elevate in all aspects of your life. Remember, transformation and renewal should not end here; they should be a daily regimen in your life. Keep striving towards your own personal spiritual elevation and know that this is not a one and done. Go through the processes in this book as many times as you find it necessary. I believe you will see the beauty and blessings that come with your willingness, discipline and diligence to elevate.

Elevation- Transformation = Stagnation

Thoughts Of Virtue

Moving Forward

_____

_____

_____

_____

_____

_____

_____

_____

_____

_____

_____

_____

_____

_____

_____

_____

_____

_____

_____

_____

_____

_____

_____

_____

_____

_____

_____

_____

_____

_____

_____

_____

_____

_____

_____

_____

_____

_____

_____

_____

_____

_____

_____

_____

_____

_____

_____

_____

_____

_____

_____

_____

_____

_____

_____

_____

_____

_____

_____

_____

_____

_____

_____

_____

_____

_____

_____

_____

_____

_____

_____

_____

_____

_____

_____

_____

_____

_____

_____

_____

_____

_____

_____

_____

_____

_____

_____

_____

_____

_____

_____

_____

_____

_____

_____

_____

_____

_____

_____

_____

_____

_____

_____

_____

_____

_____

_____

_____

_____

_____

_____

_____

_____

_____

_____

_____

_____

_____

_____

_____

_____

_____

_____

_____

_____

_____

_____

_____

_____

_____

_____

_____

_____

_____

_____

_____

_____

_____

www.ingramcontent.com/pod-product-compliance
Lightning Source LLC
Chambersburg PA
CBHW060518130626
46553CB00002B/557